"They just told me the P.A. system is not working, but they've discovered the problem. There's a screw loose in the speaker."

Mid 1960's, Electric Coop meeting. "Did you know that Benjamin Franklin married a redheaded widow and discovered electricity?"

IBM meeting, Austin Texas. "We had a terrible day at the office. Our computers shut down and we all had to think."

Demand on the speaking circuit forced Doc Blakely to learn how to fly in order to make his engagements. In 1974, he left his college teaching job to "Soar With Eagles." He quips, "I'm only nervous between take-offs and landings."

A 3,000-hour, instrument-rated pilot, Doc gives the traditional "thumbs-up" sign after an appearance before the International Flying Farmers Association.

The famed Knife and Fork circuit required speakers to dress in tuxedos. "Cut yourself shaving and you'll look like a wounded penguin."

With friend and fellow speaker, Bob Richards, Olympic decathlon champion.

Speaking at the British Columbia Sports Hall of Fame, the night the legendary Terry Fox was inducted as the Athlete of the Year in Canada. Two standing ovations and an encore showed Canadian appreciation of humor. "I'm not an athlete, but I do have the fastest mouth in the south."

Chicago, largest Rotary club in the world. "Mark my words. Women will be admitted to Rotary. Nobody should be discriminated against simply because of the shape of their skin."

Granddaughter, Torie, in front of the Alamo, has her heritage explained. The Blakely clan is a mixture of Scottish and Choctaw Indian bloodlines. "My great, great grandfather was an old Indian fighter. My great, great grandmother was an old Indian."

"I speak at grass fires, goat ropings, feeder pig sales, and at other high-class functions like these."

Robert Henry (L), Joe Griffith, and Jeanne Robertson—Doc Blakely's colleagues in the Platform Professionals speakers' group. It has been said that "Laughter is the hand of God lifting the burdens from the shoulders of a troubled world."

Doc's Seminar "How To Keep Yourself Indispensable" is a fun program covering communication, goal striving, human relations . . . and lots of laughs.

Doc's national headquarters is located here in The Loose Goose
Saloon. "My lawyer friends come here to study for bar exams."

Executive skills are practiced behind a hand-carved, self-designed
desk. "I bring in a bunch of the neighbor kids to applaud when
it's time for me to quit for the day."

When the Yellow Ribbon Co. wanted to have a Bavarian theme in Minneapolis, Doc Blakely obliged at the meeting planner's request. For this photograph, he also confiscated a bottle of Schnapps and the Fraulein pouring it.

Extroverts can't resist getting involved with the audience . . . Wisconsin Farmers.

On the national television show, Nashville Now, Doc gets his share of the laughs. "A hurricane came through my hometown of Wharton, Texas. It did $250,000 worth of improvements."

Roger Miller and Doc Blakely horse around back stage. "King of the Road" Miller quips, "This photograph should be a boost to the old career . . . huh, Doc?" Blakely replies, "I sure hope it helps you, Roger."

Fellow Texans—Freddy Fender and Doc Blakely—study a television script. "I'm thinking of adopting a stage name, Freddy. What do you think of 'Herbie Hubcap'?"

Doc is author or co-author of three humor books. "This one has become a million seller. I've got a million of 'em in my cellar."

In Wharton, Texas the most important question on people's mind is "Who has the double six."

Invitations to speak in Hawaii, Bermuda, Jamaica, Mexico, and cruise ships are not uncommon. Doc and wife Pat are shown here fighting over a pineapple in Honolulu. They were rehearsing for a 1988 tour of New Zealand for a large insurance company.

Explaining how hairstyles change as you grow older—"Let's not dwell on the negative. I may be loosing my hair, but you've got to admit I've got nice teeth."

The ultimate award for contributions made to the field of professional speaking is the "Cavett." The ninth recipient of this prestigious award (1987), Doc Blakely joined an elite group so honored by his peers in the National Speakers Association. Even then the humorist couldn't resist, "You know what this means . . . No more working with agents!"

DOC BLAKELY'S HANDBOOK OF WIT AND PUNGENT HUMOR

James "Doc" Blakely

Rich Publishing Co.

Houston, Texas 77070

First Printing 1980
Second Printing 1983 (Revised Edition)
Third Printing 1988 (Revised Edition)

Library of Congress Catalog Card No.
83-61029

ISBN 0-9607256-2-8

(Previously ISBN 0-13-216861-8)

Printed in the United States of America

FOR
PERRY, KIM, TORIE
AND
MIKE, BECKY, ERIC

Table of Contents

How This Humor Handbook Will Make You a More Dynamic Speaker

There is a magical ingredient that when added to a speech is one of the most powerful attention-getters known to mankind—humor. The average audiences expect speeches to be dull, they anticipate boredom by an unimaginative dialogue. Humor, if skillfully handled, works wonders. But let's face it, much humor is not skillfully handled because too many speakers think laughter is precipitated by a long, drawn out joke that may, in reality, turn out to be just as boring as a dull monologue on the population growth statistics of the snail darter.

The important question is, "Where does one find humor that will be appropriate, to the point, short enough to prevent boredom, and funny enough to excite the laughter mechanism?"

Doc Blakely's Handbook of Wit and Pungent Humor answers that question with over 1200 entries categorized by 92 subjects and cross-referenced to ease your search for that special pungent line or joke.

This book is a collection of two special types of humor widely used successfully by the professional

speaker or story teller. One form is the short, quick, one-
or two-liner, usually used to add pep and zest to everything from an entertainer's act to comedy relief in an
otherwise serious presentation.

The other type is a condensed form of the humorous
story, known far and wide as the joke. Who has a use for
this material? If you read, write or speak the English
language, you will find an encyclopedia of appropriate
humor for any occasion.

In addition to the thousands of witty lines, a special
feature of this book—RX for That Ailing Speech—gives
you 81 specific tips on how to best use a story, what can
go wrong and how to prevent that from happening,
where to use it, when to include it, why it works, and a
host of helpful pointers. More than a humor collection,
this is a *handbook* of a unique collection of material and
techniques. For example, read entry 14, imagine how
you might use this line. Then read RX #1 for a discussion on how a professional thinks when he is considering a story of this type. Note also that both the entry and
the RX are "bare bones" material or instructions. As
Shakespeare wrote, "Brevity is the soul of wit." The key
element of the soul of *Doc Blakely's Handbook of Wit and
Pungent Humor* is that no words are wasted. It gets to
the point quickly.

Scattered throughout the more than 1200 humorous entries, you will also find humor philosophy (RX
#17), therapy (RX #52), inspiration (RX #78) and
scores of other aids to successful use of quick wit.

The entries are arranged alphabetically by categories ranging from Ads to Women. Finding material is
simple and fast, reduced to three logical methods. First,
consider the subject category—banks, for instance—and
look up the page number for that category. Secondly,
after studying the entries, note additional references, by
bold entry number, at the end of most sections. Thirdly,

make your own list of associated thoughts connected to the business of banking (loans, accounts, credit, etc.) and refer to the index for a rapid referral to other ideas. Weave these lines and stories into your existing material and you will find yourself coming closer to speaking perfection. RX #7 also explains further use of the listing method to combine forms of humor drawn from the contents and index.

Keep in mind that the lines and jokes in this book are purposely written in a timeless style so that they remain fresh. As a speaker, performer, conversationalist or writer, you have the opportunity to provide the most important ingredients—personality, timing and freshness. In order to keep your material current, simply take the timeless material in this handbook and modify it to include names or topics that are currently in vogue. Presto, you produce local, state, national, international humor that is far superior to the latest stale jokes that are still making the rounds.

For still further assistance, after selecting your pungent lines, try reading the 81 tips, numbered separately for your convenience, under the headings RX for That Ailing Speech. By referring to these equally short musings, again and again, new ideas, hunches and inspiration will leap into your thought processes. The key to the use of any handbook is to use it often. Repetitive usage leads to greater retention and deeper understanding. After experimenting with the material and ideas in this handbook for a few months, you may even decide to do what I do with it. I keep a copy at my office, one at home and one permanently packed in my travel bag. And I *write* in all of them, making additional notes or references to material that is of special value or interest to me.

Many good humor books are on the market. This one is unique. In addition to the more than 1200 pungent entries, it is equally fast to use in *searching* for that special line or joke. All that and 81 tips—RX for That Ailing Speech—make it a must for the student, master or admirer of the art of producing smiles, chuckles and laughs.

My own qualifications for serving as a tutor to lovers of humor through this accumulation of material are quite simple. I am both a professional speaker and writer. As a professional humorist on the after-dinner circuit, I am expected to deliver a witty and polished performance. It is not only an expectation, it is a necessity since my livelihood depends upon pleasing an audience, mainly through good, clean humor. Since I am invited back to address some audiences many times, it is essential to have a depth of material on which to draw. My reputation on the convention and business circuit is at stake every time I perform.

My personal philosophy has always been to develop a sincere, important or worthwhile message and say it as humorously as possible with no vulgar or off-color stories. Any student of humor recognizes that the most difficult form of humor is the use of the clean, wholesome story. It is much easier to make an audience laugh through the use of "blue" material. Listeners often respond to this kind of material out of nervousness or embarrassment rather than glee. For this reason, my humor collections have had to be of extremely good quality in order to reach my personal goals and still maintain my personal livelihood.

As a professional writer of humorous material, I find the same need for quality word imagery.

All the material contained in this book is from my own personal collection of quips, quotes and jokes which I have judged fit to keep, for use as it is, or to stimulate my imagination to develop original material. Most of these lines have been tried many times on live audiences across the nation. You can be assured that every thought received close scrutinization by a full-time professional humorist before it was judged good enough to keep.

As a professional humorist who has not been exposed on television, the material offered in this book is still relatively fresh, and I offer it to you to make of it what you will. I have used it to make a comfortable income, both in the verbal and written form, along with a pleasant way of life for many years.

James "Doc" Blakely

How to Use Wit and Pungent Humor to Add That Touch to Your Speech

"What do you do for a living?"

"I'm a professional after-dinner speaker."

Strangers put the question to me daily. The reaction is inevitable. The jaw slackens, the eyebrows jerk upward as if attached to the hands of a puppeteer, the scalp tightens at the ears, there is a faintly audible gasp of inhaled air as the head jerks in my direction.

Swift revolve the wheels of intense thought, and keen interest can be sensed as the next question forms in the mind of the inquirer. The answer is so simple that I am repeatedly surprised at the obvious concentration of the questioner anticipating the response.

"Is there a secret to holding the attention of an audience well enough to become a professional?"

My answer is more in the form of a three-part plan, a simple map guaranteed to yield verbal treasures for those willing to prospect until the trail ends at the podium of performance. It is there that the end of the rainbow surely rests on a wealth of satisfaction not unlike the mythical pot of gold. And remember that rainbows are invisible except to those who either by accident or design are in the proper position to see refracted light. At this moment you hold in your mind's eye the power to see all the colors in the spectrum.

STEP ONE

"First of all," I reply, "it is necessary to be prepared so thoroughly for a presentation that it appears to be ad-libbed." This is the first step on the path to effective humor. Spontaneous wit is always appreciated by an audience because they believe that there is no way other than quick thinking to respond to a sneeze in the audience with, "Bless you sir. I do hope your condition isn't as serious as my Uncle Fred's. He died from a sneeze … He was in another man's closet at the time." Spontaneous? Far from it. Unexpected, yes, but thorough preparation gives the pro the option of making an audible call at the line of scrimmage to face the changing situations. The mind is a vast computer, able to recall in fractions of a second material programmed to be retained. But where do you get the material? You study every source, read every article, listen for it in every conversation, sense it in the silent depths of your own thoughts. Then you discard 99 percent of your research and program your computer only with the material that fits your game plan, practicing until every thought can be recalled microseconds before it is needed or planned. With over 1200 one- or two-liners and jokes, this book is a collection representing only one percent of that considered during years of listening, studying, writing, thinking, and trying out material on live audiences.

An old adage among humorists is "If you want a 20-minute speech, tell 20 jokes; a 30-minute speech, tell 30 jokes." If this material only resulted in ten percent retention, by your own standards you would have enough preparation for a two-hour speech according to the old adage. Some comedians pay writers fifty dollars or more for one good line that may last only 10 seconds. On that basis, using only the ten percent solution to preparation, this book represents a $36,000 value. But let's be realistic. It probably has much more than ten percent hidden in the spectrum of ingredients that refract the light of thought for those who will position themselves and focus beyond the immediate horizon to see the rainbow and where it leads. It will not be easy to accomplish, but the treasure map and instructions are simple and clear whether you use humor exclusively or sparingly; the treasures care not how they are spent. A friend once described a book to me by saying, "There was something on every page that could be underlined and used. If you just took the ideas from one page and followed through on them it was worth the price of the book." Students of humor will see the value in this, and many other published works in the field, and make it a part of their preparation. Drawing on many sources is also a sure-fire way to freshness.

STEP TWO

"Secondly," I continue, "a program chairman hires professionals not only because they come prepared, motivated to perform, but because they can deliver with great timing." Many speakers subscribe to the theory that timing is not only the most important thing, it is everything. But how can you have great timing if you have no material, or less than you should, and the computer banks of your mind are gathering dust? Timing depends on a wealth of material, delivery without noticeable delay, riding the crest of attention, enthusiasm or laughter and following it with wave after wave of continuous assaults until the tide of thoughts overtake the beachhead of listeners and retreats in its own good time. Just as each drop of water makes up the vastness of the sea, each bit of material adds force to your verbal tide sending out sprays of wit, refracting light to bridge the gap between speaker and audience with a colorful rainbow leading to the spot where X on the map marks the third and final point. Call it a chest of gold or treasures of the mind, it is real, it is visible. The combination lock to this treasure chest is opened by imagination.

STEP THREE

"Imagination," I say with a glint in my eye that Rudyard Kipling would envy, "is the third factor that separates the pro from the crowd, a combination of many thoughts, humorously phrased, woven into a word picture that is revealed to everyone in the audience at the same time." Imagination in speaking refers to combining and recombining ingredients of speech material into a workable formula, a secret recipe of your own. Imagine this—only four one-liners have sixteen possible arrangements in an order of presentation. With the over 1200 lines, jokes, and stories contained in this volume, the arrangements are astronomical, limited only by the power of your imagination to work the right combination that will unlock your personal treasures.

This verbal treasury is a mixture of one- or two-liners and short jokes along with hints on how I have used them to best advantage. The entire collection is filled with one- or two-liners, quickies, little jewels that add sparkle to your crown of glory, arranged alphabetically by subject. There is also a standard form of the joke, the timeless utilization of a tale with a sudden surprise, the ending skillfully concealed until the last possible moment. A good joke, in keeping with the theme or subject you are speaking on, carries your message on the wings of humor to a height of retention difficult to match by all but the most charismatic serious speaker. Combine material of your own choosing and you can build a personalized string of jewels designed to keep the mind moving along the desired treasure path, rewarding it frequently with one- or two-liners and giving the full measure at the end.

The One- or Two-Liner

Virtually every speaker in the country, amateur or professional, can use this highly effective form of communication on some occasions. A few professional humorists rely on it entirely.

Although not all of them will be covered here, several ways of utilizing these quickies exist.

If you are simply entertaining an audience, the mood can be set with a simple theme such as "It's possible." Then, unleash as many unrelated quips as desired. Don't be afraid to try them. Your audience will be the judge of their effectiveness and, as long as they are forewarned, won't mind in the least that there is no continuing connection between thoughts.

If you want to present a very professional-type job, memorize the selections and know them well enough that a fair acting job makes them appear to be random thoughts that pop up in your mind. To prevent heart failure (your own), try each piece of material on one or several persons before using it on a crowd. One simple way is to replace the familiar greeting to friends of "How are you?" with "Have you heard the thought for the day?" Then lash out with something like "The President brought a new spirit into the White House and his brother drank it." Soon your friends will prompt you by asking for your thought for the day because they know it won't be long enough to be boring, at worst, and might be the happiest thought they'll hear, at best, for the next 24 hours. If you keep up your thought for the day, just imagine how much material you will have tried out in a year!

Another way to use the one-liner is to decide what theme you want to follow. A broad example is sports. Look up every subject connected with sports, such as Athlete, Football, Coach, Referee, and Physical Examination. Connect these together in the desired order and keep rearranging until you have the right, logical combination of connecting thoughts. Serious messages, jokes and stories can also be interspersed.

A reverse order for the serious, inspirational, motivational or educational speaker is to decide on the message and content, then select the desired number of one- or two-liners to add variety or spice to important subject matter. "Did you hear about the fellow who gave up smoking for health reasons? It made him so nervous that he started chewing toothpicks and died of Dutch Elm Disease. ... The loss of 100 million dollars to disease of our state's timber crop was unexpected too, but here are some basic steps to a preventive program to insure the health of our forests." Others can be used at appropriate intervals. You will be amazed at what a half dozen well-chosen one- or two-liners will do for an otherwise serious, lengthy speech.

The use of humor form has so many ways you're bound to like some of 'em. So is the audience.

The Joke

Technically a joke can be any number of things; either verbal, physical, auditory or visual, that elicits laughter. Humor analysts may go very deep into the psychology of laughter and what constitutes a joke, but let's examine it briefly here to illustrate a point. One definition of a joke is a story so skillfully told that the outcome is in doubt right up to the very end and is such a surprise that it moves the average listener to express an emotion, hopefully laughter. Josh Billings jokingly described this emotion as "a release mechanism, sort of like the lettin' out of Sunday School."

Note that the previous definition indicated a story skillfully "told." We seldom laugh out loud at something we read. The jokes in this book have been translated to a written form that is most advantageous to convey the "surprise." Get the flavor of the story from the written version, practice telling it so the complete picture is revealed, if possible, with the last two, three or less words.

You must learn to use your own style and imagination in selecting the word combination that withholds the punch line best for you. If you see a written story that you particularly like, try several ways of marketing the product to best advantage. Any joke that seems funny to you can be sold as funny to others.

But here's an important tip in using jokes. If you want to set your mind at ease about the possibility of a low level crowd reaction, always use a joke to carry a message. If they laugh, or if they don't, you have a logical reason for having told it. If the audience laughs you'll have no trouble deciding where to go from there. If they don't, you have a "saver" built in by saying something like, "I tell that little story to illustrate a point."

Let's take one complete example of how to use this handbook's joke material. Suppose you read the following:

A lady gets on an airplane with a small child. "Mom," whines the child. "Not now, son," replies the mother. A few seconds later he repeats, "Mom." "Just a minute. I'm busy." Before she could put her luggage under the seat he is at it again. "Mom," he continues. "Oh, what is it?" asks the exasperated mother. "Mom, how do lions kiss?" Rolling her eyes upward, she replies, "I don't know son. Your father is a Rotarian."

Converting that to a verbal form, a speaker will change it slightly, add physical gestures for visual effect and use is something like this:

"I was on a plane coming over here yesterday and a young woman sat in front of me. She was trying to get a two-year-old child to sleep and her four-year old kept tugging at her sleeve and saying 'Mom.'"

"Just a moment son. I'm trying to get your sister to sleep." (Speaker looks down acting out the part of the mother talking to a child.)

"Now, go to sleep honey and..."

"Mom."

"I told you just a minute ... now go to sleep honey and when you wake up..."

"Mom."

"What *is it* son?"

"Mom, how do lions kiss?"

"I don't know son, your father's a Rotarian."

"Glad to see a few proud wives at this Rotary Club luncheon. We could all take a lesson from that young lady and keep our sense of humor under trying situations."

One word of caution. Not everyone feels comfortable telling a story and acting it out as if it happened to them. The audience senses this and won't "buy" your experience. If you feel uncomfortable in that role, an alternate method is to tell it as a dream, a fantasy or simply say, "Flying can be hard on your nerves. It's like the young mother who boarded an airplane..." The audience knows right away that a joke is unfolding and gets prepared in anticipation of a fun story.

Use your imagination with the following jokes. Get the idea, add a little flavor, stir with a gesture or two and serve to all who come seeking a spoonful of mirth. Develop your own special ingredients. The recipe continues to improve with each use and the final product will feed from one to infinity.

Is there really verbal wealth in this cache of wit? Study this treasure map of humor, dig deeply at the right spot and see for yourself.

So there you have my three-step formula: preparation, timing, imagination. Add material and you're ready to travel from podium to platform. Prepare to embark on a long, pleasant journey full of surprises, grins, chuckles and laughs. Practice your timing on friends, family and audiences. Do it until it appears ad-libbed. Combine, build, tear apart, recombine imaginatively. *Prepare* the material to have the *timing. Imagine* the fun you will have. Then do it.

ADS

1. Los Angeles Ad: Young lady with can of corn wishes to meet young man with can of lima beans. Object—Succotash.

2. A manufacturing plant in Nashville advertised for workers on their midnight to eight "graveyard shift." The ad read: HELP US MAKE IT THROUGH THE NIGHT!

3. A daily newspaper featured these advertisements: On sale in bargain basement: Shirts for men with minor flaws and shoes for women with slight imperfections.

4. An ad in local newspaper: Wanted: Go-Go Girls. No strings attached.

5. "Last week I ran an ad in the newspaper for a husband," said the spinster, "and I got lots of replies. They all said, YOU CAN HAVE MINE."

6. Classified Ad: Wanted—job in dynamite factory, chemical plant or other highly inflammable explosive area. Trying to quit smoking.

7. Classified Ad: For Sale: skis. Used once. For information phone Room 111, County Hospital.

532, 1000, 1085

AGE

8. The old guy who just turned 104 said that if he had known he was going to live so long he would have taken better care of himself.

23

9. Grandpa says that what this country needs is some way of freezing all the excess energy a man has when he's 18 so he can thaw it out and use it when he's 80.

10. The only way to live to a ripe old age is to cut out everything that makes it worthwhile.

11. You've entered the Golden Age when the silver in your hair turns to lead in your pants.

12. That "difficult age" for women is when they are too young for medicare and too old for men to care.

13. Young men look forward, old men look backward and middle-aged men look terrible.

14. I know a man who is so old that he has lived through three revivals of the wide necktie.

15. The most irritating fellow at most high school reunions is the man with only two things—money and hair.

16. When an elementary teacher had a birthday recently, her class joined in the observance. "How old are you?" the students wanted to know. She gave the conventional answer—39. A boy in the class pondered awhile and then said, "I don't see how you could be 39. My father's 50 and you taught him in the 7th grade."

17. Wife: "What makes you think you're getting old?"
Husband: "Women my age are starting to look good to me!"

18. Sam, of Miami, was 80 but wanted to have a good time before he died. He dyed his hair black, got silicone shots in his cheeks, went to a gym to work out, bought some mod clothes and a brand new car. He came upon a good-looking widow, close to 40, and they were driving around, happy as could be, when a bolt of lightning struck Sam. When he reached heaven, he cried: "Why me,

God?" And God answered: "I'm sorry, Sam, I didn't recognize you."

19. The town's oldest citizen was interviewed by the press on his 96th birthday. In addition to the usual questions asked as to what he attributed his longevity, one reporter asked the oldster how he felt when he woke up in the morning. His answer: "Surprised."

20. At a big New Year's Eve party, an attractive matron asked a young man to guess her age. "You must have some idea," she said as he hesitated. "I have several ideas," he admitted with a smile. "The only trouble is that I can't decide whether to make you 10 years younger on account of your looks, or 10 years older on account of your charm."

RX for That Ailing Speech

RX #1. It is important to keep in mind that a punch line is connected to a certain situation. It would be extremely difficult to get a laugh from material unrelated to the current train of thought in the minds of an audience. But if the material is connected in some way with the meeting, or better yet, with an incident that the audience realizes could not have been a set up, it becomes even more humorous.

You can predetermine some of the remarks by guessing at what will happen at the meeting in question. For instance, if there is to be a meeting of senior citizens or a committee on study for the advancement of aging, any of the previous remarks could be held ready and used at the appropriate moment. The main thing to remember in using short one-liners is to make them appear as if they were ad-libbed. Then when it comes your time to speak, simply throw out a few one-liners and connect them with what has previously been said. It will take a little practice to learn how to weave the material together, but the results are worth it.

Here's an example. Suppose a man was introduced at the meeting on study of the aged who appeared to be in excellent health and very vital but was in his 90s. The crowd is obviously impressed. When it comes your turn to speak, simply point out the gentleman and say that you are amazed at his excellent condition but imply that you are not surprised at his age because you heard him remark earlier that he had lived through three revivals of the wide necktie. Don't bother about asking his permission to pull his leg. His reaction may trigger a greater response than the remark. The element of surprise works in your favor best if you're the *only* one who knows where the line is headed. One precaution—make sure he is robust and healthy or with an obvious sense of humor.

*   *   *   *   *

21.   He's not only over the hill, he's clear down the other side.

22.   Some women grow old gracefully—others wear stretch pants.

23.   He's at that sad time of life when he'd rather not have a good time than have to recuperate from it.

24.   I wouldn't say he is old, but I can tell you that his Social Security number is 2.

25.   I don't mean to say he's old, but when he was a child the wonder drug was Mercurochrome.

26.   Old? He has enough wrinkles to use his face as a snow tire.

27.   There comes a moment when a mirror tells a man that he has more chins than a Chinese phone book and his lap appears amputated. That's when he starts to improve his mind ... or lose that too.

28.   Three ages of man: youth, middle age, and "TRY TO READ MY LIPS."

29.   A pious Jew who reached the age of 105 suddenly stopped going to the synagogue. Alarmed by the aged man's absence after so many years of faithful attendance, the rabbi visited his venerable congregant. Finding that his friend Mendel was still in good health, the rabbi asked, "How come after all these years you stopped coming?" "I'll tell you, rabbi," the centenarian said, "when I reached 105 I figured that God must have forgotten about me—and I don't want to remind him."

30.   A man in England decided to visit a married couple he hadn't seen for some time. The wife opened the door. "Hello, Maggie, nice to see you," he said. "How's Jim?" "Jim?" she repeated. "Didn't you know? He's dead. Went down to the garden to pull a cabbage for dinner and as he bent down he fell dead right there on the spot." "How terrible!" exclaimed the visitor. "What on earth did you do?" She answered, "Well, what COULD we do? We had to open a can of peas!"

31.   A neighborhood squabble brought several housewives to court, each eager to tell the judge why the whole thing was somebody else's fault. "One at a time, ladies," said the judge. "You'll each be given a chance to testify. I'll hear from the oldest among you first." The case was dismissed for lack of evidence.

RX for That Ailing Speech

RX #2.   Careful now, because all of the previous remarks mostly involve an insult type of humor. You must be kind enough or such an astute judge of character that you do not embarrass someone with one of these quips. The study of human nature is perhaps more important to your survival as a humorist than the humor used. Learn to judge people. There is no need to ask permission to rib someone in advance because this destroys some of the spontaneity of the situation. However, if you will take time to get acquainted with people in the audience, you will invariably run into the "character" and it is not difficult, with a little practice, to select those people that you know will not be offended by your remarks. Just in case, however, always smile when you use some of these rather cutting barbs. An added suggestion is to make a little gesture with the hands to indicate that you are sort of waving away that remark. If you are uncomfortable with this type of humor, simply use your imagination to twist the comment around and tell it on yourself. Your audience will love you for it.

*   *   *   *   *   *

32.   At twenty, we don't care what the world thinks of us; at thirty, we wonder what it does think of us; and at forty, we realize we started thinking about it twenty years too late.

33.   The man who is old before his time must have had some time before he was old.

34.   You're over the hill and way down the slope when you can't even remember what it is you're worried about.

35.   EARL WILSON: "You're getting older when your favorite part of the newspaper is '25 years ago today.'"

36.   He's at the age that when he gets out of the shower, he's glad the mirror's fogged up.

37.   You're still young if the morning after the night before still makes the night before worth the morning after.

38.   You're never too old to learn, unless, of course, you're a teenager.

39.   We are only young once. That is all society can stand.

40.   An aging beauty queen still thinks her face is her fortune. If that's true, she ought to sue her banker for a loan.

41.   The peak of mental activity must be between the ages of 4 and 17. At 4 they know all the questions; at 17, all the answers.

42.   When an elderly man was asked why he refused to eat Jello, he replied, "I don't want to eat anything more nervous than I am."

RX for That Ailing Speech

RX #3.   The last two comments (entries 41 and 42) make a beautiful example of the range a humorist must have. The story concerning the peak of mental activity is a cutting remark at young people. The Jello story jumps to the other end of the scale. You must be smart enough to recognize that these stories often will be humorous only if they are given in the reverse situation concerning age groups.

In other words, a teenager audience is not as likely to find the remark concerning "knowing all the answers at 17" very humorous. If it is a mixed audience containing parents and teenagers, however, they will invarably catch and share the joke. The Jello story may find some acceptance by an elderly audience, but it is most appropriate when you have an audience that is approaching retirement but still rather mentally young and vigorous. Humor has a way of relieving the tension of facing the inevitable situation of growing old.

* * * * * *

43.   The best thing about getting old is that all those things you couldn't have when you were young, you no longer want.

44.   He thought old age was creeping up on him, but it turned out to be cheap underwear.

45.   Respect Old Age—especially when it's bottled.

617, 717, 720, 948, 1045

AMERICA

46. America has a great industrial-military system. We've sent arms to everyone but the Venus de Milo.

47. An Englishman, thrilled at his first visit to America, stepped off the ship in New York and gazed around at the tall buildings. Stopping a passerby, he said, "I can scarcely believe I am in America. Is this really New York City?" The man smiled, nodded and said, "Si, senor."

48. If you want to know why Americans are thought to be strange, just flip on the evening news. All over the world people are worried about the Middle East, earthquakes, famine, floods. What are we worried about? How to feel really safe under our arms!

49. The Modern American drives a bank-financed car over a bond-financed highway on credit-card gas to open a charge account at a department store so he can fill his savings-and-loan-financed home with installment-purchased furniture.

50. "Beastly place," an Englishman said as he was flying with an Irishman and an American over the Sahara. "The devil's home," the Irishman commented. Speaking last, the American declared, "What a parking lot!"

51. What America really needs is an electric blanket crossed with an electric toaster alarm so we could pop out of bed every morning.

52. America can be defined as: Cab drivers with baby shoes dangling from the windshield. Cleaning women paid by the hour who talk about their arthritis. Men in cocktail lounges who ask if you live nearby. Landlords who grin while you are signing the lease. Old friends who ask you to co-sign a loan. New friends who ask you to co-sign a loan. Strangers at parties who ask your astrological sign. Saloons with pay toilets. People at dinner parties who ask if you're in the phone book. Rich women with chalk-white skin, red cheeks and blue hair. Singing bus drivers. Meter maids with crepe-rubber shoe soles. TV repairmen who scratch their heads in disbelief even before they have examined the set. Banks that send literature welcoming you to the neighborhood. Waitresses who call you "doll" within the first two minutes.

53. Americans: The only people on earth who have mastered the art of being prosperous while they go deeper in debt.

54. If America is not a nation of gamblers, how come less than half the babies born in this country are planned?

55. Probably America's greatest energy conservationist was Christopher Columbus. He got 3,000 miles to the galleon.

RX for That Ailing Speech

RX #4. Here's an important point in speaking, especially humorous speaking. Every word must be distinctly pronounced so that the audience gets the image immediately. Nearly every joke is a joke only as long as the punch line can be concealed until the last possible instant. If you mumble the punch line or stumble on the timing of your joke, you loose some effectiveness, perhaps all effectiveness.

For instance, one of the previous stories (entry 55) concerns Christopher Columbus. When my secretary first typed this, my comment was misread. It turned out this way, "Probably America's greatest energy conservationist was Christopher Columbus. He got 3,000 miles to the gallon." This isn't funny—it does not make sense and projects no image. When I caught the mistake, I had it changed to read correctly. See if you get the point when just one tiny letter is added to a story. "Probably America's greatest energy conservationist was Christopher Columbus. He got 3,000 miles to the galleon." If you understand the meaning of galleon, you get a completely different picture.

Just as leaving out a letter in a written story changes the meaning of a joke, so leaving out a syllable or not speaking distinctly enough can destroy your material. In other words, if you use this line, be sure to pronounce "galleon" plainly, but don't make the terrible mistake of going too far and saying "gall-e-on." This implies that you didn't think the audience was intelligent enough to catch the joke in the first place so you spelled it out for them.

*   *   *   *   *   *

56.   We, in America, should all take a lesson from the girdle. It won its popularity by being able to adjust itself to any circumstances.

57.   How can America live with feet, fathoms, furlongs, acres, B-cups, petite and extra large and be confused by the metric system?

58.   If you are ever asked what America stands for, you might answer, "Too much!"

59.   There are several things to show that America is in good shape—the GNP, the drop in unemployment and the blonde bending over at the watercooler.

60.   If there's no divine plan for America, how come just enough happens each day to fill up the six o'clock news?

61.   Talk about equality! Where else but in America could Phillis Diller be the same sex as Farrah Fawcett?

62.   In Russia, they banish the writers when the challenge the leaders. In America, we banish the leaders who then become the writers.

ANIMALS

63. Always follow the example of a duck: Keep calm and unruffled on the surface but paddle like crazy underneath.

64. For nearly a year, it was rabbit for dinner, or beans. Then suddenly our aim seemed to go haywire. We began missing easy shots and couldn't understand why. Was our ammunition bad? Or had our guns gone flooey? We learned by accident why we were missing those rabbits. Those old cottontails had got smart. They'd started going around in pairs with their heads three inches apart. Then when they saw the beam of a flashlight, each rabbit closed its outside eye!

65. STEVE ALLEN: "Asthma doesn't seem to bother me any more unless I'm around cigars or dogs. What would bother me most would be a dog smoking a cigar."

66. A man took a dog into a bar. He ordered drinks so he and the dog could have a quiet conversation. The bartender bet the man $20 that the dog couldn't talk. Others took a piece of the action. When the dog just sat there, the crowd took his money, booted him and the dog into the street. "Why didn't you talk?" asked the guy. The dog replied, "Are you kidding? Can you imagine the odds we'll get tomorrow night?"

67. Agriculture and education go hand in hand. They say you can lead a mule to water but you can't make him drink. That's true, but you can rub a little salt on his lips and make him thirsty.

68. A herd of buffalo was charging down the range when the leader stopped abruptly and the other buffalo pulled up behind him. One of the herd shouted at him, "What'd ya stop for?" the leader replied, "I think I just heard a discouraging word!"

69. Maybe an elephant never forgets, but, after all, what does it have to remember?

70. His dog is so dumb, he has a flat face from chasing parked cars.

71. The great thunder god was riding the winged horse Pegasus across the heavens shouting, "I'm Thor! I'm Thor!" And Pegasus replied: "I told you to uthe a thaddle, thilly."

72. Two dogs were fed a bowl of boiled okra. One grabbed it and it went down so fast he thought the other ate it so he bit him.

73. Hear about the big game hunter who quit going after elephants because the decoys were getting too heavy for him?

RX for That Ailing Speech

RX #5. Note that the last quip in this section (entry 73) concerns a big game hunter and the punch line is not withheld until the very last as is the usual rule. There are exceptions to every rule and perhaps this is one of them. The story just does not flow as well if it is worded so that the last word releases the image. This story will not be a "biggie" but it can be used extremely well as a "set up" to convey a more serious point.

For instance, I would use this story knowing that the audience would not fall on the floor over the hilarious nature of the tale, but would follow it up with something like, "All of us on occasions are subjected to carrying a heavy load. At times like these we need to throw off the burden by looking at the more ridiculous side of life. Now here's our vice president in charge of marketing." You have completed three missions with this bit of nonsense: (1) Allowed the audience to groan *at you* (who knows, they may even laugh), (2) Delivered a bit of philosophy which they can appreciate, (3) Set them up for a better story when they expected none, *plus* getting the market expert off on the right foot. What the vice president does after that is up to him/her.

*   *   *   *   *   *

74.   Did you hear the story about the dog that walked into a flea circus and stole the show?

75.   WILL ROGERS: "A fellow ought to live his life so he wouldn't mind loaning the family parrot to the town gossip."

76.   A clipping from the Bryan County, *OK Star*, all about cows: "A cow is a completely automatic milk manufacturing machine. It is encased in untanned leather and mounted on four vertical, movable supports, one on each corner. The front end contains the cutting and grinding mechanism, as well as headlights, air inlet and exhaust, a bumper and a foghorn. At the rear are the dispensing apparatus and an automatic fly swatter. The central portion houses a hydrochemical conversion plant. This consists of four fermentation and storage tanks, connected in series by an intricate network of flexible plumbing. This section also contains the heating plant, complete with automatic temperature controls, pumping station and main ventilating system. The waste disposal apparatus is located at the rear of this central portion. In brief, the external visible features are two lookers, two hookers, four stander-uppers, four hanger-downers, and a swishy wishy. With all that equipment, you'd think a cow would bring a little more money."

77.   Let's play horse. I'll be the front end and you just be yourself.

78.   The next time you call your dog a dumb animal, remember who he has working to support him.

79.   The old maid who had a male dog entered him in a dog show. But she made a mistake and entered him in a female class. "Did your dog win a prize?" a friend asked. "No, he didn't, but it was my fault," the old maid said. "I had him entered in the wrong class." "Was he commended?" the friend asked. "No, he wasn't commended, but I tell you right now, he was delighted."

80. I saw a bumper sticker that read: HELP PRESERVE OUR FOREST ... SHOOT A WOODPECKER!

81. There is no education in the second kick of a mule.

82. A man took his Great Dane to a veterinarian and said, "Doctor, you've got to do something. My dog does nothing but chase sports cars." "Well, that's only natural," the vet replied. "Most dogs chase cars." "Yes," the man agreed, "but mine catches them and buries them in the back yard."

83. "I'm going to enter Fido in the dog show next month."
"Do you think he will win many prizes?"
"No, but he'll meet some very nice dogs."

84. For future Thanksgivings, farmers should develop a turkey crossed with a kangaroo. It'd be the first turkey in history you could stuff from the outside.

RX for That Ailing Speech

RX #6.   In the case of animals, they may be joked about in a variety of situations. They lend themselves well to *associations* that deal in some way with animals. For instance, a restaurant association, a veterinary group, a leather manufacturing company, a chemical company that makes pesticides, a pharmaceutical branch that produces livestock drugs, even clothing manufacturers are involved in the animal world in some way. It is but a short connection to make humorous groups relate to the stories previously listed. And of course, wildlife associations like Ducks Unlimited are a natural for some of the above quips. The key to using any of this material is to tie it to a relevant situation. Take the last story for instance—it could be used at any Thanksgiving gathering but would be even more appropriate for a meeting of biologists who happen to be meeting on or near Thanksgiving day.

* * * * * *

85.   A pronghorn antelope can jump 20 feet ... provided he's followed closely by another pronghorn antelope.

86.   Hear about the cowardly horse thief who stole only a Shetland pony? They hanged him just a little.

87.   Confucious say: "Duck who fly upside down must quack up."

88.   A fellow went to dinner at a friend's apartment on the 17th floor of a Manhattan apartment house. While his hostess attended to some last-minute details in the kitchen, he played with her German shepherd. He threw a rubber bone several times and the dog went to fetch it. Then, throwing harder than he intended, he threw the bone out the terrace door and over the railing. Incredibily, the dog followed it out to the terrace and bounded over the railing to the street, 17 floors below. Horrified, the young man began pondering what to say. When they finally sat down to dinner, he looked at the hostess and said, "Perhaps it's just my imagination, but your dog seemed rather depressed tonight..."

89.   A fellow said to the veterinarian, "Something's wrong with my horse. One day he limps, the next day he doesn't. What should I do?" And the vet said, "On the day he doesn't limp, sell him!"

90.   Every morning for 11 years a man awakened at six and took his dog for a walk. Suddenly the dog died. The next morning the fellow woke up at the same time, stared at the ceiling for a moment, then nudged his wife. "Hey," he said, "you wanna take a walk?"

91.   A city friend just back from a dude ranch has made the dandy observation that a duck is a bird that walks as if he had been riding a horse all day.

> **109, 110, 111, 112, 113, 114, 116, 117, 118, 120, 122, 123, 124, 125, 131, 194, 264, 384, 386, 410, 559, 808, 991, 1041, 1047, 1050, 1052, 1065, 1192**

ARABS

92.   Let us all now ponder the question, "Do Arab women dance sheik to sheik?"

93.   You can always tell an Arab because when he gets out of bed, he takes the sheet with him.

94.   Latest news out of the defense department is that to maintain the balance of power in the Middle East, the U.S. will sell Israel phantom jets and the Arabs will get real ones.

95.   Those Arabs really have us cornered. They're taking the money they get from us for their oil and investing it in solar energy.

96.   Those Arab sheiks have so much money they don't know what to do with it. One of 'em just ordered a custom-built Rolls Royce and took his change in Pontiacs.

97.   But how about the Arab oil sheik with fifty wives who died waiting to get into a bathroom.

BACHELORS

98.   Any man who thinks there is no such thing as a good loser is probably no longer a bachelor.

99.   A bachelor never makes the same mistake once.

100.   "Why haven't you ever married?" the party hostess asked the eligible bachelor. "Well, I'll tell you," he replied. "I'd rather go through life wanting something I didn't have than having something I didn't want."

101.   Advice to bachelors: Marry a girl from Moscow. She'll be happy, lovable and used to following orders. Besides, your mother-in-law will live in Russia.

102.   A trust fund handles all your money without having to follow your advice. It's a service for fellows who don't have a wife.

103.   Every bachelor hates to see the beaches close and the girls in their bikinis leave because he knows his eyes are on their last legs.

627

RX for That Ailing Speech

RX #7.   One of the tricks of the trade for the humorist is to use the short one-liners, such as some of the material used in this book, as "asides." Asides are little bits and pieces of material that add color to a story before releasing the major thought or punch line. Here's a helpful hint for using asides such as those covered under the general heading of "Bachelors." Take a standard joke with a punch line. Nearly every individual has some favorite story that they love to tell. Most often these good-natured tales are long, drawn out, involved jokes of the standard variety. Here's a way to spice them up and get a lot more mileage out of your humor while still retaining the confidence of using an established joke:

Think of your favorite joke that revolves around marriage (bachelors, husbands, wives, mothers-in-law, etc.). Now simply tell the story, including as many of the comments under bachelors as you can that will fit into some logical sequence in the story. In this way, your audience is constantly rewarded with little hors d'oeuvres before you deliver the main course message. Here's an example of a standard joke with the normal punch line followed by the use of "asides" to fill out the story, making it a unique version for you.

There was a man who was extremely henpecked but developed enough courage one day to stay after office hours for a few rounds of drinks with the boys. Naturally, since he had been denied this recreation for so long, when he got a few drinks under his belt, he let it go to his head. He came home in the wee hours of the morning, walked up to the door, braced himself and was just about to bang on the door to have his wife let him in the house. As he went to pound on the door, she jerked it open and he fell flat on his face in the hall. He just rolled over, propped up his head on one hand and said, "I believe I shall dispense with my opening remarks and just answer questions from the floor."

Now here is the same story utilizing some asides to get numerous laughs, and if they don't, you haven't lost anything during the course of the telling of the tale:

"I once knew a fellow who made the mistake of getting married and became very henpecked. He had a problem that most bachelors don't have. A bachelor never makes the same mistake once.

"He got enough courage to stay late after office hours and drink a little with the boys down at the local bar. He got so looped that he told the fellows he wished he had married a girl from Moscow. Then he wouldn't be henpecked because his wife would be used to following orders. Besides, his mother-in-law would live in Russia.

"It didn't take him long to run out of money because the other fellows also convinced him to buy most of the drinks because most of their assets were tied up in trust funds. That's a service for fellows who don't have a wife.

"He finally left the bar in an inebriated condition arriving at the front door of his house about 2 a.m. He was suffering from a condition that usually only happens to bachelors when the beaches close at the end of the summer ... when the girls disappear over the horizon in their mini-bikinis. That is to say his eyes were on their last legs.

"Just as he went to pound on the door, his wife jerked it open and he fell flat on his face. He rolled over on one elbow, propped his head on his hand, looked up at her with those bloodshot eyes and said, "I believe I shall dispense with my opening remarks and just answer questions from the floor."

Note that all these "asides" were drawn from the entries under "Bachelors." The same thing could be done using other related entries such as husbands, wives, marriage, etc. You are limited only by your imagination.

BANKS

104. He swears by his bank. Its deposits are insured by the U.S. Government and its toasters are guaranteed by the Japanese.

105. He's so overdrawn at the bank that the manager asked him to give back the bank calendar.

106. My cousin was fired because he couldn't leave his work at the office. He was a bank teller.

107. A small town bank gained title to a filling station via a foreclosure. To show his interest, the bank president sent one of his loan officers to the gas station to check the operation. The loan officer decided to get the feel of the business by helping at the pumps. When his first customer said, "Fill 'er up," the loan officer started to spring into action, but then asked the customer: "How far are you going?" "Just down to the state line," the customer replied. "Then you won't need a full tank," cautioned the banker. "I'll let you have five gallons."

108.   Sign in a Chicago bank: "If any bank says they're friendlier than us, we'll punch them in the nose."

272, 388, 748, 752, 771

BIOLOGISTS

109.   A biologist crossed a gorilla with a porcupine. He doesn't know what he has got, but it has stopped beating its chest.

110.   A green biology student crossed a rooster with another rooster and got two very cross roosters.

111.   A biologist tried to raise an orphan porcupine with a wire brush for a surrogate parent. The little fellow backed into the brush and asked, "Is that you, mother?"

112.   A biologist crossed a gorilla with a computer and got a Harry Reasoner.

113.   A biologist crossed a elephant with a mole and got really big holes in his lawn.

114.   A biologist crossed a skunk with an owl and got something that smells but doesn't give a hoot.

115.   Hear about the biologist who is trying to cross a computer with a rubber tree? He hopes to come up with a computer that will make snap decisions.

116.   Hear about the biologist who crossed a cow with an elk and now he has a place to hang the milk pail?

117.   Hear about the biologist who crossed a bird and a ball point pen? He got a woodpecker with a retractable beak.

118.   Hear about the biologist who crossed a broom with an octopus? He got a bale of hay with eight handles.

119. Hear about the biologist who crossed a sponge with a potato? Tastes terrible but it holds lots of gravy.

120. Hear about the biologist who crossed a mink with a gorilla trying to get a cheaper full coat? The sleeves were too long.

121. Hear about the biologist who crossed poison ivy with a four-leaf clover? He came up with a rash of good luck.

122. Hear about the biologist who crossed a pigeon with a statue? It couldn't get off the ground.

123. Hear about the biologist who crossed a carrier pigeon with a woodpecker? The bird not only carries messages but he knocks on the door.

RX for That Ailing Speech

RX #8   Here is a good place to bring out a rule that most amateur humorists have come to recognize by intuition. Occasionally the rule may be broken, but usually it is best left in the hands of the professional to do so. I refer to the rule of three. It is generally accepted in humor that one general theme is overworked after it has been attacked three times with punch lines that are quite similar. This seems to hold true for most jokes as well. If you think back to a situation joke, the story almost always involves deceiving the mind by making at least two dead end attempts and releasing the punch line with the third try. In the case of one-liners, the same rule can apply. However, make each attempt a punch line because of the shortness of the quips. In other words, try any of the biologist one-liners previously discussed in any order you desire. It is best to save your strongest punch line for the third spot. It is even appropriate to select a story that is mediocre or even weak as the first quip so that the momentum will build.

For instance, using the rule of three and some of the random remarks previously discussed, try building your own story such as the following: "Here about the biologist who crossed a sponge with a potato? It tastes terrible but it holds lots of gravy (weak story for beginning). This same guy crossed a mink with a gorilla and got a cheap fur coat but the sleeves were too long (momentum builds some here). He crossed a bird with a ball point pen and got a woodpecker with a retractable beak (this should be the strongest punch line in these three examples).

If you follow this up with any more than three, chances are that the surprise element will continually decline and the audience will begin to groan because you have overdone a clever routine. The key to the whole thing is to try your own arrangements until you get the proper audience response. Nobody can tell you if a story or a combination of stories is going to go. The audience will let you know after some experimentation and then you will wind up with proven material that is your own combination.

* * * * * *

124.   What happened when the biologist crossed a swordfish with a giraffe? He got a terrific tree surgeon.

125.   The Georgia biologist, in preparing for Thanksgiving, crossed a turkey with an ostrich, figuring he'd get something with monstrous drumsticks. Instead, he wound up with a queer bird that runs over and sticks its head into the mashed potatoes.

BORN LOSER

126.   That guy's a born loser. He's a newcomer in town and was run over by the Welcome Wagon.

127.   My uncle is a born loser. He got a wooden leg and it developed varicose knotholes!

128.   You can't win for losing. Did you hear about the guy who quit smoking cigarettes to guard against cancer? He took to chewing on toothpicks and died of Dutch Elm disease.

129.   He's a born loser. He took a gal to the Tunnel of Love and she made him wait outside.

130.   A born loser was standing on the edge of Echo Cliff. He yelled, "Hello, I'm Milfred Merriweather." Echo came back, "J-U-M-P."

131.   All of my life I've been a born loser. I ask you— who else has a parakeet with bad breath?

132.   A born loser is a guy who comes to a halt at a stop sign, looks both ways, then is hit in the rear.

296

BOSS

133.   The boss complained to the new office boy who was half an hour late, "You should have been here at nine o'clock." The kid asked, "Why, what happened?"

134.   A cowhand was called on the carpet for cussing the ranch foreman. The boss asked, "Did you call him a liar?"
"Yep."
"And did you call him stupid?"
"Yep."
"Did you infer that he was an opinionated, **pompous egomaniac?**"
"Nope ... but would you write that down so I can remember it?"

135.   Our boss went to see a psychiatrist. As he emerged from the doctor's office, someone asked him how it went. Our leader glanced back at the shrink and said, "Oh, he'll be all right!"

136.   A bus driver was interviewed. "I don't want you to be reckless or take the slightest chance," said the boss. The driver replied, "I'm your man, can I have my salary in advance?"

137.   There are only two sides to an argument with the boss—his side and the outside.

138.   The boss only expects us to work half a day ... and he doesn't care which 12 hours we choose.

RX for That Ailing Speech

RX #9.   Although you may not be a professional humorist or have any inclination to become one, the philosophy of humor can be utilized by nearly everyone who can appreciate a good story or the use of humor in an appropriate situation. These short quips lend themselves especially well to the business world in alleviating a dull presentation. At every conference, convention, seminar, company report, service club meeting, anywhere that people gather, the audience expects to be bored a large percentage of the time by dull speakers. This is especially true when someone reads their speech.

If you have to make a rather boring report or read a dull company policy or program, try using some of the material in this handbook to liven up the report. One bit of philosophy that could apply well is the old rule of thumb used by some professionals: *Tell one joke for every minute of your speech.* The professional humorist or joke teller can get a lot more mileage out of a piece of material because he is adept at building images and keeping the audience laughing during that minute until he reaches the climactic point at which the audience explodes. Although you may not want to be that entertaining, or have need to be, you can still use the philosophy.

Because these quips are so short, the average one-liner will take up only a few seconds. However, by utilizing one of these for every minute of your prepared speech, you can inject 30 witticisms during the course of a 30-

minute presentation and the audience will suffer less, enjoy you more and listen more closely than you think. Therefore, the suggestion is to write out your report; then for every minute of time taken in giving your report, inject a one-liner that relates in some way to the subject at hand. For instance, if you are giving a financial report and the company has suffered a temporary loss of revenue, as compared to last year, use some of the born loser stories. It can be as simple as this: "We suffered a temporary loss in revenue because of plant expansion in this area last year. We are not born losers in this company, however, and expect this to improve greatly next year. You know what a born loser is? That's a guy who comes to a halt at a stop sign, looks both ways, then is hit from the rear. We expect to go forward."

*   *   *   *   *   *

139. My boss said I was so busy when needed that I was described as being about as useful as a parachute in a submarine.

140. The boss was concerned about the cashier at his nightclub who drew special attention because he never said a word during the three weeks he had been working there. When the boss lost his temper, he hit the employee in the mouth and out popped $43 in quarters.

141. The boss has been telling everyone he held the rank of Ship's Optician in the Navy. What he really did was scrape the eyes out of potatoes.

142. Employee to Boss: "I'd like to have a raise, sir. I'm worth more than I'm getting." Boss to Employee: "Of course you're worth more than you're getting Morton. Why don't you let up a bit?"

143. Two exasperated bosses were talking about an undependable hand. "How long has he been with us?" one asked. "He has never been with us," the other replied sadly. "He has been against us from the start."

144.   The boss says experience allows you to recognize a mistake when you have made it again.

145.   The new computer turned out to be too big to fit in the company's elevator. "How am I going to get this thing to the third floor?" the deliveryman complained. The boss saw no problem. "Plug it in—and let it work it out for itself."

146.   "Boss, can I take off? It's our silver anniversary." "Okay, but am I going to have to put up with this every 25 years?"

519, 522, 633, 1018, 1055, 1169

BRIDES AND GROOMS

147.   An old chestnut refers to the bride who told her husband she wanted to stop at two children. When he asked her why, she said that she had read that every third child born in the world was Chinese.

148.   Did you hear about the groom who surprised his bride with a slinky, black negligee? She had never seen him in anything but boxer shorts.

149.   If you are what you eat, most bridegrooms are both under-done and burned to a crisp.

150.   Boss: "Why do you want two weeks off?"
Employee: "I'd like to accompany my bride on her honeymoon."

151.   Mae West: "There are two kinds of girls—those who neck and bridesmaids."

152.   A bride in her wedding gown was seen running across the golf course to a fellow about to tee off. On her way over he yelled at her, "I told you, only if it rained."

153.   The beauty of marrying an ugly bride is that in 20 years she'll be as pretty as ever.

154.   An amorous suitor won his blushing bride with this little jewel: "I won't be happy till your voice leaves the whole world the way it leaves me ... weak and limp."

623, 649

RX for That Ailing Speech

RX #10.   A great deal of selling humor to an audience is involved with "acting out" the situation. Take the lines from above for instance. This will not be as funny to an audience as it could be unless the teller uses his expressions and physical demeanor to add to the punch line. The first few lines of the amorous suitor should be spoken with the chest thrown out, the eyes lifted upward and perhaps the hands and arms extended as if to embrace the object of his affection. In this position you would recite the lines: "I won't be happy till your voice leaves the whole world the way it leaves me." Then a slight pause and the actor slumps his shoulders, drops his hands and arms along with his head and replies in a faltering voice, "weak and limp." Learn to use your body as well as your voice and mind to sell an audience on the proper image and you'll get a lot more laughs.

BUSINESSMEN

155.   A businessman and his partner closed their office and went to the movies. While there, one nudged the other and gasped, "Gosh, Joe, we forgot to lock the safe." "What's the difference," asked the other. "We're both here, aren't we?"

156.   Behind every successful businessman there stands a surprised mother-in-law.

157.   A businessman instructed his secretary to write a letter to a business friend in Buffalo and make an appointment for a meeting in Schenectady. "How do you spell Schenectady, Mr. Smith?" the secretary asked. "Why, the idea? Don't you know how to spell Schenectady?" the boss complained. "I'm sorry I don't." "Why, er—Oh, well, never mind." the boss said. "Just tell him I'll meet him in Albany."

158.   There are three kinds of businessmen: successful, unsuccessful and those who give lectures telling the second group how the first group did it.

159.   A businessman told his son, "Ethics are essential to success. For example, an old customer paid his account today with a $100 bill. After he had left the shop, I discovered he had given me two $100 bills stuck together. Immediately a question of ethics arose: Should I tell my partner?"

160.   It's really a tough world for the American businessman—every time he comes up with something new, a week later the Russians claim they invented it, the Japanese make it cheaper and the Arabs buy it.

CARS

161.   What this country really needs is a car that runs on smog.

162.   "Hello. Yes, we have service trucks. Your car won't start? Well, all our trucks are out and there are several calls ahead of you. It will be at least two hours ... You say you're a doctor? Doc who? Oh yes, I remember. My wife called you when I was sick in bed with the flu. Tell you what, doc, walk to the nearest station, get two quarts of oil for the car, cover the motor with a blanket. Call me in the morning if things haven't improved."

163. Those little foreign cars have made it possible to hit a pedestrian not only below the belt but below the knees.

164. "Why do you have XYZ 123 tattooed on your back?"
"That's not a tattoo. That's where my wife ran into me while I was opening the garage door."

165. What's so different about the new cars? It still boils down to a body, a motor and a loan.

166. A guy comes into his house screaming at his wife what a lousy driver she is; she has just run over his golf clubs. Without batting an eye, the wife stares at him and says: "I told you not to leave them on the porch."

167. We just saved $18 a week on gas—we hid the kid's car keys.

168. A classic putdown was heard while a man was waiting for a fill-up at the gas station during subzero weather. The phone rang and the owner swore under his breath and mumbled, "Another service call!"

169. How far a young man goes these days depends on how much gas his father left in the car.

170. General Motors has come up with another car. It's not successful yet, though. According to one GM engineer, William B. Larson, if the car is crashed into a solid barrier at 50 mph (equivalent to hitting another car at 100 mph), all the occupants will be killed—although some only slightly.

171. My car is just like me—it's middle-aged, needs new parts, drinks, smokes and can't get started in the morning.

172.   Finally, when he had to call the wrecker for the tenth time, he remarked to his traveling companion as the wrecker came into sight, "Well, here comes my lemon-aide!"

173.   After your teenager gets through with the family car, be sure to adjust the rear view mirror, the seat position, let out the seat belt, reposition the radio station, then head for the nearest gas station.

RX for That Ailing Speech

RX #11.   Here's a good example of building the proper image so that the humor can build. If you will analyze entry 173 you will see that the joke is not as much a matter of words as a conveying of images.

Everyone has entered a car after someone else has driven it and found minor adjustments necessary. Also, everyone who has a teenager can recognize the images being projected, very quickly relating to them in parable form. If you readjust the mirror, you recognize that a smaller driver has been in your car. The seat position immediately implies that you are longer legged than your teenager. When you let out the seat belt, it implies that you have gained a great deal of weight while the slim, trim young driver is put in a more favorable light. The repositioning of the radio station immediately brings to mind the generation gap and is funny simply because the audience visualizes a long-haired youth listening to a rock-and-roll station while you, the reserved conservative, would much prefer a more sedate form of music. The final butt of the joke is you again because with all of your powerful adult position, you cannot control the gasoline consumption of one of your own children.

These kinds of stories hold a lot of humor because everyone has experienced the same thing. They are laughing not only at you because you are dumb enough to be taken advantage of by an adolescent but they are also laughing at themselves because they have experienced exactly the same thing.

* * * * * *

174.   My car has an engine in the rear. Before my wife drove it, the engine was in the front.

175.   A young man walked into a car dealer's showroom and was taken aback by the price tag on a compact car. "Why that's almost the price of a big car!" he exclaimed. "Well," said the salesman, "if you want economy, you've got to pay for it, Mister."

176.   Some American cars won't start until you hook your safety belt. In Japan, their cars won't start until you take off your shoes.

177.   "I've just discovered oil on our property," a man told his wife. "Marvelous!" the wife said. "Now we can buy a new car!" The husband set her straight: "No, we'd better get the old one repaired. That's where the oil is coming from."

178.   Being poor is having people look at your car and wonder if anybody was hurt.

179.   Filling out a questionnaire for the National AAU track and field championships, Olympic distance runner Duncan MacDonald listed his hobby as "taking apart my Volkswagon." Asked to list his ambition, MacDonald wrote, "Being able to put my Volkswagon back together."

180.   The cost of any auto repair is equal to the sum of the parts, all of your fears, and double the estimate.

181.   It's only a question of time before Detroit chooses between safety and economy—a body from Greyhound or the engine from some other dog.

182.   The patrolman asked the driver how he was involved in an accident. "As I backed out of the garage," the driver explained, "I hit the garage door, ran over our son's bicycle, tore up the lawn, rolled over our cat's tail, smashed the curb, hit our neighbor's house, creamed a stop sign, and crashed into a tree." "Then what happened?" the patrolman inquired. "Then I lost control of the car," the driver answered.

183.   What this country needs is a car that won't go any faster than a driver can think.

184.   There's a new model car on the market that won't solve the safety problem, but may save the owner money. It's painted red on one side and yellow on the other. If you have an accident all the witnesses contradict each other.

185.   Announcement: There is an emergency in the parking lot. The lights of a Lincoln Continental Mark IV were left on and the Volkwagon in front of it is beginning to melt.

186.   There are two things that must be kept in good running condition—cars and pedestrians.

> **96, 377, 419, 454, 513, 540, 639, 785, 848, 966, 1059, 1087, 1222, 1245, 1246**

RX for That Ailing Speech

RX #12.   There are many times when material (cars, for example) can be used in a situation that would probably escape the average lay speaker. For instance, how many times have you heard the MC for a program announce that somebody's car is blocking another car, headlights are left on, or some similar situation. A clever MC can build a bit of humor by fabricating a crisis in the parking lot. Everyone expects this to happen and will be listening closely to find out if the car in question belongs to him or her. A clever MC could use the quip about the Lincoln Continental Mark IV (entry 185) to gain attention from the crowd then launch into several of the other lines about cars as a buildup to an introduction of a political personality. Not only would he get laughs, but he would also gain the attention and respect of the audience and the person running for public office. Just before the politician is introduced, he could use the line, "There are two things that must be kept in good running condition ... cars and pedestrians. Here is a third thing that keeps in good running condition, our State Senator, John Brown."

CHILDREN

187. A little girl spoke loud and clear: "I pledge my allowance to the flag of the United States of America, and to the Republic for Richard Stands, one naked individual, Oh my God, with puberty and justice for all."

188. A young man was visiting his girlfriend and stayed too late. Her dad got impatient and said, "I can't see why that bird visiting Alice doesn't have enough sense to go home." "He can't go daddy," said little brother, "sister's sitting on him."

189. A little girl asked her mother if all fairy tales began with "Once upon a time." Her father answered, "No, this year they start with, 'If I am elected.'"

190. There was this six-year-old girl, who was raised on a farm and came to visit her grandmother in the city. Before she left home, the six-year-old was told by her mother that Granny was sort of old-fashioned about language. "Don't tell Granny that you have to go to the bathroom," said the little tyke's mother. "Just tell her that you have to go powder your nose." So the six-year-old came to visit Granny, and they had a great time. When at last it was time to leave, Granny told her: "You've been a nice little guest. And next time you come, you'll have to bring your little brother with you." "Oh, I couldn't do that!" protested the tyke. "He still powders his nose in his pants."

191. A child was overheard to say, "My dad has been bragging that we have a telephone in our car ever since mom hit a phone booth."

192. A kindergartener was asked what the colors of stop lights mean. The kid blurted out, "Red means stop, green means go, and yellow means swear."

193. A housewife heard a knock on her door and opened it and there stood two little boys. One of them was holding a list in his hand. "Lady," he said, "me and my brother are on a treasure hunt. Do you have three grains of wheat, a sheet of toilet paper and a pork chop bone?" She replied that she was fresh out of those things. "That's a hard list," she said. "What treasure hunt is this?" "Well," said the boy, "if we find everything on this list, we win a dollar." "And who is going to give you the dollar?" she asked. "Our babysitter's boyfriend."

194. After the death of her cat, a little girl was consoled by her mother, "Morris is in heaven now." The kid said, "Gee, Mom, what would God want with a dead cat?"

195. Asked the child: "Why doesn't Daddy have hair on his head?" "Daddy thinks a great deal, dear." The child mulled this over and then wanted to know, "But, Mummy, why do you have so much hair on your head?" "Hush—and eat your breakfast!"

196. An amazing thing about a child who takes no for an answer these days is that he bothered to ask in the first place.

197. Boy: "Mama, what did Daddy mean when he called the girl he saw on the beach a live wire?"
Mother: "He meant, Junior, she was wearing very little insulation."

198. Samuel Clemens' notes go back to the time Clemens was a boy, constantly in trouble because of his mischievous ways, so much so that his mother felt deep anxiety about his welfare. Clemens said she told him in her later years "At first I was afraid you wouldn't live long. Later, I was afraid you would." On another occasion, after Clemens had been saved from drowning for about the sixth time, Mrs. Clemens met a family friend who asked, "Weren't you worried about Sam in this latest scrape?" She said, "Oh, no! A boy who is bound to hang isn't going to drown."

199. Days of chivalry are not dead. Nowadays when a girl drops a textbook in class, there's usually a boy who'll kick it back to her.

200. A small boy was asked by his mother where he was going. He mumbled "Fishing." She asked, "What have you got in your mouth?" "Worms," said the little boy. The mother screamed, "What are you doing with worms in your mouth?" "You told me not to get my pockets dirty," explained the little boy.

201. Becoming bored on a long auto trip, a small boy suddenly said to his father, who was behind the wheel: "I wish you'd let Mom drive. It's more exciting."

202. An old Chinese proverb says, "If thine enemy has wronged thee, buy each of his children a drum."

RX for That Ailing Speech

RX #13. Here is a key point. Much humor is based on something that was originally dangerous, exciting, potentially disastrous or frustrating. Children fall into nearly all of those categories and most audiences that are old enough to become parents, regardless of current age, can relate to stories on children. Art Linkletter has based a career on the antics of children and his material is almost always a sure-fire hit. Take a hint from a professional and develop some of your own stories, arranged in some order that is convenient for you or relative to the situation at hand.

For instance, the story concerning the old Chinese proverb would probably bring the house down if a rock-and-roll band has just completed a rousing performance. Even though the audience may have enthusiastically embraced a great show, your timing in making the remark can bring out the humorous aspects of a loud presentation, especially if there is a drummer in the group. (What rock-and-roll band doesn't have one?)

* * * * * *

203. Early to bed and early to rise makes a man healthy, wealthy and likely to meet his children just getting home.

204. If you think your children don't know the value of money, try to borrow some from them.

205. A preschooler with considerable TV-watching experience wasn't stumped for a remedy when her mother lost her voice with a bad case of laryngitis. "You've lost your sound, Mama!" diagnosed the child. "Maybe you need a new tube."

206. When a teacher asked the little boy if he were animal, vegetable, or mineral, he answered proudly, "Vegetable, I'm a human bean."

207. A little boy came home from playing baseball with a disgusted look on his face. When his father asked him what was wrong, he replied, "I was traded." "That shouldn't make you feel bad. All the big baseball players get traded." said his father. "I know," replied the boy, "but I was traded for a glove."

208. There is a rumor that blacks are bearing the burden of school integration; so to soften the burden, the

Supreme Court has ruled that, for the next five years, all black children will be born to white parents!"

209. Nothing makes a new baby so homely as not being yours.

210. The young first grader had never had a physical examination before entering school. The doctor asked him, "Have you ever had any trouble with your ears and nose?" "Sure," answered the boy, "they always get in my way when I take off my T-shirt."

211. Anyone who thinks Americans don't get enough exercise doesn't have preschool children.

212. One night, Jimmy's parents paused outside his bedroom door and listened to him say his prayers. He ended up with: "God bless Mom, God bless Dad, and Grandma," and then added: "And please take care of yourself, God, because if anything happens to you we're all sunk."

213. Breathes there a child that doesn't wonder why Dad grows gray and Mom grows blonder?

214. A new Sunday School teacher had to iron out some problems with the Lord's Prayer. One child had to be corrected after repeating, "Howard be thy name." Another youngster prayed, "Lead us not into Penn Station." Still another surprised the teacher with, "Our Father, who are in heaven, how'd you know my name?"

215. Two small brothers were watching TV. Just as the Western came to a climax, with the hero facing the fastest gun in the West, the five-year-old turned off the set. "Why'd you turn off the TV?" demanded his older brother. "Cause I gotta go to the bathroom and I don't wanna miss nothin'."

216. My five-year-old may have developed more insight than error with his version of the Lord's Prayer.

He says, "Forgive us our trespasses, as we forgive those who press trash upon us!"

RX for That Ailing Speech

RX #14.   Entry 216 is a beautiful example of a story that has great flexibility in it's use. This story would fit into many categories and be appropriate to tell provided you have the creative imagination to link it to the meeting at hand. For instance, the story would fit well with teachers of kindergarten, child psychologists, religious meetings, law enforcement agencies and sanitary disposal meetings. If you study the story closely, you will see the connection to all of these groups. As an example, a spokesman for striking garbage men could probably get more press coverage by using this story than by making a plea to the general public for more money. A follow-up might be "We don't want to press trash upon the public, but we have no choice. We have five-year-old children too and if we want to support them, we will have to have either more money or another type of work. You know the old saying 'GAR-BAGE IN, GARBAGE OUT.' You get what you pay for."

*   *   *   *   *   *

217.   "John," called the mother, "tell your sister to come in the house out of the rain." "I can't Mom," the boy called back. "And just why can't you?" demanded his mother. "We're playing Noah's Ark, Mom," explained the boy, "and she's the sinner."

218.   What a shame it is that the people who really know how to bring up children are never parents.

219.   The pert eight-year-old was being punished and sat in the corner of the dining room at a table set especially for her. The rest of the family paid her little attention during her term of penitence, but they couldn't ignore her praying before settling down to the meal. "I thank thee, Lord," she was heard to say, "for preparing a table before me in the presence of mine enemies."

220.   The boy had a point when he asked his mother,

"Why is it when you're worn to a frazzle, I'm the one who has to take a nap?"

221. A five-year-old boy knocked on the door of a neighbor's house. The four-year-old girl who lived there answered in her nightie.

> Boy: "Can I come in and play?"
> Girl: "My momma says little boys should not see little girls in nighties." Then she slammed the door. The boy stood there wondering what to do when the door opened and the little girl said, "You can come in now. I've taken it off."

222. Small boy: "Mommy, they say I look like a monkey!"
Mother: "Shut up and comb your face!"

223. A little boy said to his teacher, "I'm going to be an astronaut when I grow up." "Do you really want to fly in space?" asked the teacher. "No," admitted the little boy. "I just want to go eight days without a bath."

224. A mother asked her son, "Do you know what happens to little boys who lie?" He answered, "Yeh, two years before the other kids, they get to see X-rated movies."

225. The new family in the neighborhood overslept and the six-year-old missed the school bus. Mother, though late for work, agreed to drive him if he'd direct her. They rode several blocks before he told her to turn the first time, several more before he indicated another turn. This went on for 20 minutes, yet when they finally reached the school, it proved to be only a short distance from their home. Asked why he'd led them over such a circuitous route, the child explained, "That's the way the school bus goes, Mom, and it's the only way I know!"

226. A little girl put all her dolls in her carriage and sighed, "I don't know how I'll manage. I'm expecting again at Christmas."

227. Little boy meets little girl. She has an apple, which gives him an idea. "Let's play Adam and Eve." said the little boy. "How do you play that?" asked the little girl. "You tempt me to eat your apple and I'll give in," explained the little boy.

228. Children are unpredictable. You never know how high up the wall they're going to drive you.

147, 706, 778, 798, 903, 993, 1147

COLLEGE

229. There once was a college football star who didn't give girls a second thought. The first one covered everything.

230. I graduated from State College. It recently changed its name. They used to call it a cow college, but not it's just an udder university.

231. Attending college seldom hurts a man if, when he graduates, he is willing to get an education.

232. "Is your son making it in college?"
"No. I'm making it. He's spending it."

233. American education is now wide open. Where else could you have a son studying to be a nurse and a daughter at West Point?

234. The president of a university explained in a recent speech that the president of a university is supposed to do the speaking for the school, the faculty members are supposed to do the thinking and the purpose of the dean is to keep both from doing either.

235.   "The college I attended certainly turns out some
great men."

"What year did you graduate?"

"I didn't graduate—I was turned out."

526, 531, 622, 681, 1089, 1122, 1125

RX for That Ailing Speech

RX #15.   Most people have difficulty in coming up with humorous anecdotes because they simply do not make the necessary mental connection in advance of the situation where the humor will be used. Suppose you are to make a presentation on a college campus. A logical place to start would be humor covered in this handbook under college. However, there are not enough lines to cover the subject thoroughly so you have to improvise. Make a list of all the subjects that could be connected with a college and you will readily see where other information can be gleaned to fill out your humorous remarks. Just by reading the few remarks contained under "College," your list could grow to include football, basketball, coaches, girls, cheerleaders, education, agriculture, money, budgets, nurses, military, presidents, teachers, administrators, etc. The list is staggering once you let your imagination lead you from point to point.

The key to successful humor is making the "bridge" between one subject and the next. A bridge is simply a structure that allows the traveler to overcome an obstacle in his path. Bridges of humor may be built on such foundations as time, age or geography. For example, here is a geographical connection. "I've heard that this is a very sophisticated college. Real Ivy League. The southern college I went to was mostly bush league. You never saw so many people in the bushes. But here in the midwest things are different. I talked to a boy today who is studying to be a nurse and a girl who is trying to get into West Point."

Another example would be: "Colleges out west are different from this one. Many of them have changed from a cow college to an udder university. However, midwestern schools are in the conservative part of the country. In spite of that, I understand your dean came from liberal New York. You know the purpose of the dean up north, don't you? The president speaks for the college, the faculty members think for it, and the dean keeps both from doing either."

Notice that every "bridge" was a geographical connection. Other bridges of time, age, era, religion or nationality could be just as effective.

CONGRESS

236. A congressman had a nightmare—dreamed all that money he was spending was his.

237. Congressional leaders are cautious about a tax cut. They say it's not something you rush into ... like a congressional pay hike.

238. Transcendental meditation, by the way, consists of sitting down, closing your eyes and letting your mind go blank. Congress has been practicing it for years.

239. The cost for sending congressmen abroad wouldn't be so bad, but they keep coming back.

240. If you should meet up with a well-dressed stranger in Washington and want to know what he does for a living, ask him to show you the photos in his wallet. If the pictures are of a woman and children, the man could be unselfish, honest and intelligent. If the pictures are likenesses of himself, then the bearer is undoubtedly a congressman.

754

COOKING

241.   One good thing about cooking outdoors. It keeps the flies out of the house.

242.   A traveler told an East Texan he had a great recipe for baking a ham. "What you do," he said, "is you put the ham in a deep pan and for one whole day you soak it in rye whiskey. On the second day you add a bottle of Jamaican rum and you cook it a while. On the third day, you add a bottle of port wine. On the fourth day, a bottle of bourbon and then you finish cooking it. How does it sound?" "Well," said the deep East Texan, "I don't know about the ham but it sounds like the makings of mighty good gravy."

243.   "What's cooking?"
"Nothing, it's just lying there thawing."

244.   "My best recipes are Irish stew and apple fritters."
"Which is this I'm eating?"

245.   "Sam, a burglar in the kitchen is eating the stew I made."
"Go back to bed. I'll bury him in the morning."

246.   The secretary, on the phone, explained that all the food editors were at home eating their own cooking, or preferably someone else's. "Well, perhaps you could help me," said the man. "What kind of wine do you serve with hog jowl?"

247.   She: "I plan the meals and slave over the stove for you every day, and what do I get? Nothing!"
He: "You're lucky. I get indigestion."

248.   My wife makes a mean party dip. It's an old recipe from the savages of the Amazon who used to dip the tips of their arrows in it.

249.   A gourmet cook is the kind of man who is invited for an evening of wine, women and song and asks, "What kind of wine?"

> **149, 266, 323, 363, 642, 650, 783, 1231, 1232, 1234**

CREDIT CARDS

250.   An extravagance is anything you buy that you can't put on a credit card.

251.   The trouble with Robert Van Bergen's credit card, issued by a San Diego department store, was that it called him Robert Vanbergen. He returned it, pointing out that there should be a space between Van Bergen. He now has a new card issued to Robert Vanspace Bergen.

252.   He's too proud to beg and too honest to steal, so he buys with his credit card and forgets to pay.

253.   A credit card is a magical bit of plastic that enables a person to buy things he doesn't need, with money he doesn't have, to impress people he doesn't know.

254.   A man had barely paid off the mortgage on his house when he mortgaged it again to buy a new car. Then he sought out a banker to borrow money on the car so he could build a garage. "If I do make you the loan," asked the banker, "how will you buy gas for the car?" "It seems to me," the man replied with dignity, "that a fellow who owns his own house, car and garage should be able to get a credit card for gas."

255.   Credit cards are what people use when they discover the buy now, pray later plan.

256.   He's thinking about getting her to undergo plastic surgery—by cutting off her credit cards.

257. One of my neighbors is having his credit card retreaded in preparation for holiday shopping.

746

RX for That Ailing Speech

RX #16. Effective humor depends heavily upon effective delivery of a line with the proper timing. Entry 257 is a beautiful example of a good story that can elicit a rousing response from an audience if it is delivered with the proper timing. The timing should be relatively fast because you want to bombard the audience with images that are rapid-fire so as to build the momentum in a strongly connected statement of current economic conditions.

A good way to practice delivering this is to pat your foot in a motion that approximates a muscian keeping time to the beat of a band. Try tapping your foot to a very slow rhythm of approximately one beat per second. Then recite the previous long one-liner in a rapid-fire delivery. Every time your foot makes a down beat, bear down on a syllable and you will soon discover a delivery technique that is very effective in a long involved one-liner such as this. It also helps to make the delivery of a long masterpiece such as this in one breath. Don't be obvious about inhaling at the start but do be obvious about exhaling at the end. This conveys to the audience the impression that you have just said a mouth full and lends to the humorous interpretation of the satire.

DANCING

258. A man fell two-thirds behind in his payments for cha-cha-cha lessons at a dance studio. The studio sent a hypnotist to his house, and when he woke up he only knew how to cha.

259. Men have given a lot of thought to the art of belly dancing among women and come to the conclusion that they would have been better off thinking about something else.

260. There's a skinny girl performing down at the belly dance review. It's easy to understand why she continues to show her navel. It's the only thing on her body which isn't flat.

261. My lodge brothers took their wives to a New Orleans dance review. The girls objected to the fan dancers, the boys objected to the fans.

262. The best thing you can say for today's dance steps is that if someone makes a mistake, no one knows.

263. Grandpa said he knows why the kids don't touch nowadays when they dance, "You don't never touch nobody who's havin' a fit!"

264. Two dogs were watching a teenage dance when one looked over at the other and said, "You know if we acted that way, they'd worm us!"

92, 506, 684, 1226

DAUGHTERS

265. The best way to get the world to beat a path to your door is not to invent a better mousetrap but to have teenage daughters.

266. Packaging has gotten so clever. This morning my daughter broke open an egg and fried a pair of pantyhose.

267. Truck Driver: "Sir, may I have your daughter for my wife?"
Father: "Trot your wife around and I'll see."

268. My daughter is looking for a man who has everything—and will part with some of it.

269. You have to feel sorry for kids. My daughter went on a diet and had braces put on her teeth. She had so much metal in her mouth, she skipped dinner, gargled with salt water and gained three pounds in rust.

270. Daughter (listening to rock music): "Did you ever hear anything so wonderful?"
Father: "The only thing I've ever heard quite like it was a collision between a truckload of milk cans and a carload of ducks."

188, 189, 205, 233, 490, 572, 1149, 1153, 1159

DENTISTS

271. There is a toothpaste that gives you a feeling of confidence. Tastes like a dentist's fingers.

272. Fellow down at the bank thinks his dentist really charges too much: "Last week he put in a crown. I think it belonged to Queen Elizabeth!"

273. George Washington had false teeth made out of wood. That's why he never smiled—afraid of attack by the English termite.

274. A dentist reports he's working on a tooth with a built-in mechanism to spray a small quantity of alum which can be fitted into an upper plate—for old codgers who have a puckering problem.

275. I like my new dentist, he's honest. A lot of guys will do some work and then surprise you with a big bill at the end. This guy took one look in my mouth and said,

"It would be cheaper to hire a dog to chew your food for you."

DEODORANT

276. Two workers: "Whew, somebody's deodorant has given out." "Well, it wasn't mine. I don't use any."

277. Now there is a deodorant that promises protection around the clock. It works, too. Notice how seldom you find a smelly clock these days.

278. A new deodorant contains a mixture of baking powder and corn starch. You get hot, perspire, and break out in biscuits.

345

RX for That Ailing Speech

RX #17. Remember the popular television show Laugh-In? One of the reasons for the success of that highly humorous format was described by one of the writers: "We throw away all the joke and just use the punch line." Laugh-In, if you recall, was virtually a series of punch lines one after another. The writers and performers of that show were successful because they literally bombarded their listeners with short, quick bits of humor.

A lot of ex-sailors probably also recognized numerous "salty" tales that they had heard during their military life. However, since the joke was not told, only the punch line, listeners were able to recall a risqué story quickly. Although the punch line may not have made sense to viewers unfamiliar with "dirty jokes," this made little difference, because the actors only consumed a brief moment before they were covering something more comprehensible. Using this method, the performers were able to reach a maximum range of interest in viewers without resorting to profanity or vulgar material. The interpretation of the story had to be purely in the mind of the individual.

This brings up a point. Do not ever use material that is vulgar, dirty, risque, insulting, humiliating or used with an intent to hurt any of your audience. The true humorist will strive to make an audience laugh without making them mad. For that reason, you will not find one single joke in this collection that has even so much as a single vulgar reference in it. If you must use questionable material, use the Laugh-In formula and throw away the joke, just use the punch line and let the listeners interpret it the way they want.

DIVORCE

279. A lady (82) wants a divorce from her husband (87) after 60 years. When the lawyer asked, "Why?" she said, "Because enough is enough."

280. Tom sued his wife for divorce because she was mean tempered, bossy and had three straight sets of twins. Grounds—she was overbearing.

281. A fellow says he and his wife are getting a divorce. "It's a friendly separation," he says. "I get to keep whatever falls off the truck as she's driving it away."

282. The worst thing about a divorce is that somewhere two mothers are nodding their heads and saying, "See, I told you so!"

283. A woman suing for divorce was seeking alimony on the grounds that while her husband was an inveterate gambler, she was an ideal wife. "Some ideal!" snorted the defendant. "I hocked the kitchen stove to play a hot tip at the track—and she didn't miss it for nine days."

284.   Judge in divorce court: "I'm going to give your wife $500 per month."

"Thanks, Judge," the man said, breathing a sigh of relief, "I'll try to help out a little myself."

641

DOCTORS

285.   A consultant is a doctor they call in to take part of the blame in case you die.

286.   A doctor got a frantic call from a housewife: "Doctor, you've got to come over at once! It's my husband! When he got up this morning, he took his vitamin pill, his ulcer pill, his tranquilizer pill, his antihistamine pill, his appetite-depressant pill, and added just a dash of benzedrine. Then he lit a cigarette—and there was this big explosion!"

287.   Doctors think a lot of patients are cured who have simply quit in disgust.

288.   A young man from the hill country was being given his Army physical examination. It was the first time any such fuss had been made over him, and he was a bit carried away by it all. The doctor was puttering around, peering into his eyes, asking questions, and writing everything down. "Have you got any scars on you?" the doctor asked. The youth was startled for a minute, but recovered. "I ain't got no scars, doc," he chirped, "but if you'll let me get my clothes I kin let you have a cigarette."

289.   A successful doctor is one who can keep his patients alive long enough for nature to heal them.

290.   When the medical man came home to find his basement flooding, he immediately called the plumber in town. The latter arrived, found and fixed the trouble in five minutes and presented a bill on the spot for $100. "Why that's outrageous!" exclaimed the doctor. "It works out to over a thousand dollars an hour! I'm a transplant surgeon and I don't make that kind of money." "Yes, I know," deadpanned the plumber, "neither did I when I was a transplant surgeon."

291.   Mary had a little lamb. The doctor nearly fainted.

292.   The doctor told a patient to strip to the waist and he took his pants off.

293.   A hypochondriac exclaimed to his doctor that he was certain he had a fatal liver disease. "Nonsense," protested the doctor. "You wouldn't know whether you had that or not. With that particular disease, there's no discomfort of any kind." "Good heavens!" the alarmed patient gasped. "My symptoms exactly!"

294.   Scientists tell us nothing is impossible. Of course, they haven't tried calling a doctor on Sunday.

295.   A woman reported that her five-year-old son and his five-year-old friend were watching television at her house. Some sort of medical-type program was on. "Why do they wear masks when they do operations?" the visitor inquired. "Because," said the knowledgeable host, "if they make a mess of it, the patient won't know who did it."

296.   When I was born, I was so ugly the doctor slapped my mother.

297.   "The pain is killing me," moaned the waiter as he lay in the emergency ward. "Help me! Help me!" The doctor eyed him coldly and told him with deep satisfaction: "This isn't my table."

298.   Expectant mother, "Well, at least the doctor can't say it's all in my mind."

299.   My doctor has never violated his oath—the oath he took years ago to become a millionaire.

RX for That Ailing Speech

RX #18.   Doctors are notorious for their poor handwriting. There is also a general belief among most people in this country that medical practitioners are getting rich off the general public. Although they work extremely long hours, are called out of every conceivable pleasure situation and probably deserve this type of compensation, the public still clings to the idea that doctors are overpaid. Although there is no real justification for this line of reasoning, it is still fertile ground for kidding the medical profession in a friendly way.

However, be extremely careful not to overdo this kind of humor, especially if a doctor is cast in an unfavorable light among his patients. The damage can be irreparable to his ego if the joke is carried on too far. On the other hand, if a group of medical people are in the audience, in large numbers, it is easier to joke about them because the audience realizes that no one would be dumb enough to make such cutting remarks in earnest in the presence of so many. The safest thing to do is to stick to subjects that are more universally accepted by everyone. Medical people will most likely respond best to jokes concerning their insensitivity to pain, their poor writing skills, their foregetfulness, even though they may be highly trained mental giants in other areas. Use "rich" jokes very sparingly and everyone will remain in good humor.

*   *   *   *   *   *

300.   A specialist is a medical doctor who has trained his patients to be ill during office hours.

301.   "My small son has swallowed my fountain pen," Mr. Green telephoned his doctor. "Please come at once." The physician inquired, "But what are you doing in the meantime?" Mr. Green answered: "Using a pencil."

302. RODNEY DANGERFIELD: "I still get no respect. I remember when I had an operation and the surgeon put a mask over my face."

303. A woman, red-faced and walking fast, brushed past an incoming patient. "What did you tell her, doctor?" asked the nurse. "Told her she was pregnant." replied the doctor. "Was she?" asked the nurse. "No," replied the doctor, "but it sure cured her hiccups."

304. My doctor is so expensive, I call him Neiman Marcus Welby.

305. "Your husband's nerves are shot. You must see that he has complete rest," the doctor told the wife. "But he won't listen to me, doctor," she said. "That's a start," the doctor said.

306. Doctors can give discouraging answers to your medical probes at cocktail parties, such as, "Sure, just undress and let me examine you."

307. Mike went to see the doctor about his wife's eyes. The doctor suggested she bathe them every morning in brandy. When the doctor saw Mike again, he asked: "How are your wife's eyes? Did she follow my advice?" "She tried to," Mike said, "but she can't raise the glass higher than her mouth."

308. The doctor in town says he doesn't believe in unnecessary surgery—he won't operate unless he really needs the money.

309. EYE DOCTOR: Please read the bottom line on the chart.
AIRLINE CAPTAIN: What eye chart?
DOCTOR: Good grief! You're an airline captain? How can this be possible?
CAPTAIN: My near-vision is okay. I can read the gauges.

DOCTOR: But what about when you're ready to land? How do you know when?

CAPTAIN: That's easy. I look over at my co-pilot. When he goes EEEEEEEEE, I come back on the wheel and set her down.

310.   There was an accident and a man was carried to his home. A doctor was called and started to care for the patient. The wife asked, "What's that stuff you're giving him?" "An anesthetic," said the doctor. "After he has taken it he won't know anything." "Then don't give it to him," said the wife. "He doesn't need it."

162, 210, 322, 472, 563, 629, 642, 1116, 1153

DRINKING

311.   Did you hear about the Colonel Sanders cocktail? Drink two and you start using fowl language.

312.   A guy kept coming home with liquor on his breath that would dent a fender within 40 yards. His wife, trying to make a point, made him get in the car and took him down to a local distillery at the graveyard shift. She explained, "You see, honey, you can't drink it all!" "Maybe not," he grinned, "but I got 'em working nights."

313.   A pal of mine lived to be 94 years old and never used glasses. He always drank right from the bottle.

314.   A man rushed excitedly into the tavern and shouted: "A lady just fainted outside! Does anybody have a shot of whiskey?" The bartender instantly filled a glass and handed it to the man, and said: "On the house." The stranger grabbed the glass, downed its contents and handed it back to the bartender. "Thanks," he said, "I always get sick when I see someone faint."

315. According to *The Indianapolis Star*, the metric system will make it hard for the fellow with too much to drink to buy more. "Imagine a drunk asking for a 750-milliliter bottle."

316. Old attorneys never get drunk. They just lose their appeal.

RX for That Ailing Speech

RX #19. For some reason drunks are always a good source of material for humor. Most people around the world conjure up an image of a humorous situation when people drink to excess. Perhaps this is because it is basically true. While there are a few people who get mean when they drink, their antics can often be a laughable matter because of their inability to coordinate their thoughts with their actions. There are numerous "lovable drunk acts" around the country and the reason for their acceptance is generally thought to be that inner thoughts released can be excused when one is under the unfluence of alcohol. Since he or she would not normally react in this way, the viewer-listener is seeing the inner personality that every individual guards to conceal.

A good key to remember in telling drunk jokes is to differentiate between *your* spoken part and the *drunk's* reaction. For instance, if you use the previously written remark: "Imagine a drunk asking for a 750-milliliter bottle." Be sure and deliver the lines in a completely sober way until you reach the most difficult word to pronounce which is "milliliter." If you slur this word the way a drunk would, you will find the image projected is much funnier than if you merely delivered the line like a straight man, a sober one at that.

* * * * * *

317. Sure cure for a hangover... "That's a wonderful girl you married last night."

318. Bloody Mary is a drink with tomato juice and vodka. Know what you call this drink in Baptist circles, where they leave out the vodka? A Bloody Shame.

319. VICTOR BORGE: "My watch tells time, the date and the altitude. Sometimes it's good to know how high you are."

320. A fellow called up a friend one morning and asked, "Did Timothy come to your party last night uninvited?" "Yes." said the friend. "Oh," said the fellow, "the curse of drink. I heard that he beat-up some of your guests." "Yes, he punched a few," replied the friend. "Oh, what liquor will do to a man. One more question—was I there?"

321. Do you know how to prevent a hangover? Get a bigger chair.

322. Tom rushed into a doctor's office, one ear bleeding, and in an obvious state of intoxication. "What in the world happened to your ear?" asked the doctor. "I bit it by accident," the patient replied. "How could you possibly bite your ear?" asked the doctor. "I stood on a chair," he said.

323. A recipe for genuine, old-fashioned, honest to goodness Kentucky eggnog is set forth in an ancient recipe book: "First, take the juice of two quarts of bourbon..."

324. On the morning after a big night on the town, a couple of cowboys were discussing their escapade. "I don't seem to recollect too clearly what went on," said one. "Was I kinda looped?" "Well, I don't know how looped you were," his buddy replied, "but I had to wheel you to the ranch on your spurs."

325. A tavern requires that customers pay for drinks when served. It's called the "Pay as you Glow" policy.

326. A group of prohibitionists looking for evidence of the advantages of total abstinence were told of an old man of 102 who had never touched a drop of liquor. They rushed to his home to get a statement. After propping him up in bed and guiding his feeble hand along the dotted line, they heard a violent disturbance from the next room—furniture being broken, dishes being smashed, and the shuffling of feet. "Good heavens, what's that," asked the visitors. "Oh," whispered the old man as he sank exhaustedly into his pillow, "That's Pa, drunk again."

327. New drink: Half tomato juice, half white lightning. It's called a blood clot.

328. During prohibition times, a dignified southern planter met a friend on the street. The friend said, "Colonel, let's walk over to my house; I have a quart of bourbon." The colonel said, "Walk, my goatee, I'll call a taxi."

RX for That Ailing Speech

RX #20.   One of the beautiful assets of stories concerning drink and drinking is that they can cast a humorous light upon a human frailty. Thus the humor can be used to illustrate the evils of drink or it may be used to shrug drinking off as of little concern in a sophisticated crowd. The interpretation of the material will depend upon your audience and how you word and deliver the material. An evangelist could use this same type of material, and often does, to illustrate to his listeners just how ridiculous a grown man can appear when under the influence of alcohol. A nightclub comedian, on the other hand, might get waves of laughter with this subject area because many of his listeners are falling under the influence, or have already fallen, and realize that they are appearing in an abnormal light but everybody enjoys the excuse to laugh with them. This is the spirit of the "loveable drunk." Be sure and maintain this environment by interpreting the stories in such a way that everyone realizes there is no malice in your heart when delivering the lines.

* * * * * *

329. A salesman has a new job—selling sponges to executives who are too shaky to hold their glasses.

330. A fellow out in the drought area is so concerned about the water shortage that he's drinking his bourbon straight.

331. Ed's deer hunting buddy, Walt, hadn't been doing so well so Ed and a couple of the other boys sharing the cabin found Walt a spot where five trails crossed. "We hid Walt in the nearby bushes and left him," Ed said. A few minutes later, a huge buck showed up. He was a trophy animal, no doubt at all. Walt sprang from his sitting position and took three quick shots. According to Ed, "By the time he got the cork back in the bottle, the deer was gone."

332. W. C. FIELDS: "A man's got to believe in something. I believe I'll have another drink."

333. "What's that pretty-looking drink you're mixing?" asked Fred. The bartender replied, "It's a Rum Dandy, made with sugar, milk and rum. The sugar gives you pep and the milk gives you energy." Then Fred asked, "And the rum?" "The rum," replied the bartender, "gives you dandy ideas about what to do with all the pep and energy."

334. I'm going to spend my tax refund at the nearest bar. That way, the economy will be stimulated, and so will I.

335. An interviewer asked Dean Martin about stories concerning his drinking. "Ridiculous," scoffed Dean. "If I drank that much I couldn't remember anything. Now what was your question?"

336. I drink to make other people interesting.

337. Three drunks hanging on a bar. One slipped to the floor and passed out. "That's one good thing about old Tom. He always knows when to stop."

338. The Paul Revere cocktail: "Drink one and you start horsing around and waking up all the neighbors."

339. A foreign visitor asked a Dublin resident, "What is the difference between an Irish wake and a party?" "One less drunk," replied the Irishman.

340. Two drunks were conversing in a bar. One said casually, "I've just made up my mind to purchase all the gold and silver mines in the world." The other fellow took a shot, drank it slowly and said, "I don't know that I care to sell."

341. Evel Knievel cocktail: "Drink one and you jump from bar to bar until you get smashed."

342. The policeman was questioning a drunk pinned under his own wrecked car, "Are you married?" "No, officer," replied the drunk. "So help me, this is the worst fix I've ever been in."

343 "What are your hobbies?"
"I like to hunt and drink."
"What do you hunt?"
"Drink."

371, 372, 383, 425, 487, 690, 956, 1042, 1060, 1194, 1209

ECONOMY

344. In layman's terms, a recession is when you have to tighten your belt and a depression is when you have no belt to tighten. When you have no pants to hold up, that's called a panic.

345. Some people's idea of economy is not working hard enough to need a deodorant.

346. Economists often say the economy will turn up by the last quarter, but what do you do when you're down to yours and it hasn't?

347. New York City finally has decided to go the economy route—taking the whitewall tires off the garbage trucks.

348. Foreign aggressors don't realize that even if they did invade the U.S., they couldn't afford to live here.

349. Society's newest evil is "economic discrimination," which, roughly defined, is what makes the dealer decline my patronage and sell the car to some undeserving jerk just because he can afford it.

350. You'll know the economy is turning around when you pass a Japanese fellow riding a Harley-Davidson motorcycle.

351. Why all the objections to Arab investments in the U.S.? A leading economist says we should have them spend all the money here, then take it all over in the interest of internal security as they do over there.

352. A cousin from back east wrote to tell me economic conditions there are so bad that the Mafia has been forced to lay off three New Jersey judges.

334, 443, 1028, 1088

RX for That Ailing Speech

RX #21. The economy is always a good subject to joke about. If it is up, we can kid the people who have lots of money, the presidents of corporations, millionaires, bankers, Savings and Loan institutions. If the economy is sliding, the humor is just as effective, if not more so, because humor is a way of saying "things are going to pot but what the heck can we do about it?" Entry 352 as you may have noticed, is a very complicated, short piece of satire. The joke involves heresay from a cousin in another part of the country, the criminal element of the underworld, as well as the old standard joke of crooked politicians. Combine all of this with money and you have a fast-paced piece of humor that is funny simply because it keeps the listeners mind jumping back and forth between so many images that are bad until the punch line reveals what we all suspect from politicians but never dare to say. The way the line is arranged, it also allows any local judges to share in the joke because we are not impuning their honesty but rather referring to some of their colleagues far removed in a distant part of the country. Of course, if you live "back east," you simply turn the story around and use it as "out west."

ELECTRICITY

353. First step in doing any electrical work: Make sure the dry cell between the ears is connected.

354. Just when automation is ready to take over, electricity got too expensive to run it.

355. A housewife was explaining to the electrician about the special wiring job she had in mind. "I want you to install a switch in the kitchen," she said, "that will connect with my husband's basement workshop. I want everything to stop dead when I call him for dinner."

356. George Washington married a widow and became father of our country, but Benjamin Franklin married a red-headed widow and discovered electricity.

921

ENERGY CRISIS

357.   Here's a way we can save Israel and solve the energy crisis at the same time. We've got to develop a piston engine that will run on sand.

358.   To give you an idea of how Charley's mind works, he thinks the solution for our energy problem is to import 200 billion tons of sand from Saudi Arabia and drill for our own oil.

EXPERTS

359.   An expert is someone who knows no more than you do but who has it better organized and uses slides.

360.   An expert is someone who is called in at the last minute to share the blame.

361.   Ask a stupid question these days and it's usually referred to a panel of experts.

362.   The word exspert should be analyzed carefully. Ex means a has-been and spert is little better than a drip.

363.   According to the experts, four persons are needed to make a good salad: a spendthrift for oil, a miser for vinegar, a counsellor for salt, and a madman to stir it all up.

364.   An expert said: "The way things are going, you've got to be crazy or you'll go nuts."

365.   An expert said if hell were turned upside down, "Made in Hong Kong" would be stamped on the bottom.

366.   An expert said: "A shin is a device for finding furniture in the dark."

367. An expert says: "Sagittarius is surrounded by a huge ring containing 40,000 trillion fifths of alcohol at 100 proof. The bad news is it is 2,000 light years away. The good news is that it's moving our way at 60 miles per second."

RX for That Ailing Speech

RX #22. Note that entry 362 under "Experts" contains a word that is deliberately mispelled "exspert." This is done on purpose to illustrate the way the human ear can be deceived by the human mind. The word expert is not spelled e-x-s-p-e-r-t but it does sound as if that is the case. Therefore, when the line is delivered "ex means a has-been," that makes perfectly good sense. However, if you said, "and pert is a little better than a drip," it would be incomprehensible, devoid of humor. But the very fact that you say "spert" makes it humorous and perhaps less than one person in a thousand would ever stop to ask themselves if this is proper pronounciation or spelling.

This brings up another important point. Many times you will read a story that does not appear to be funny. However, if you visualize using that quip with an audience in an appropriate situation as an apparent ad lib, you may be able to recognize much good quality humor through the use of that imagery. Keep your creative imagination alive and keep projecting this material into a live situation or presentation.

FARMERS

368. A farmer put up this patriotic sign: "On this site in 1776 stood absolutely nothing."

369. Farmer: "Well, sugar, now that we've struck oil, I want you to have some decent clothes."

Farmer's wife: "Nothin doin'. I've worn decent clothes all my life—now I'm gonna dress like other women."

370.   I know a farmer who has it tough. He tried to stamp out illiteracy and bruised his foot, tried to cough up the dough on a loan and gagged. So, he threw himself on the ground and missed.

371.   "How was your corn crop this year?"
"Fine. We made over 100 gallons to the acre."

372.   A conversation between two farmers: "If you had 5,000 bushels of corn and the market dropped to 50 percent below parity, what would you get?" "Indigestion," replied one. "If it was selling for 200 percent, what would you get?" "Drunk."

373.   A farmer friend says he's used to hard times. "I got nothin' from my old man. Once on my birthday, he gave me a bat. The first day I played with it, it flew away."

374.   The old farmer went into the hardware store and bought a dozen ax handles at $1.25 each. In a little while, he came back and bought a dozen more at the same price. "If you don't mind my asking," said the clerk, "what are you doing with all the ax handles?" "I'm sellin' 'em," the farmer replied. "What do you get for them?" the clerk asked. "I get a dollar apiece." "Well, you don't make much money that way." "No, I don't." replied the farmer, "but I tell ye this—it shore beats farmin'."

375.   Farming is getting so tough that two brothers were in the hog raising business and although one stole the hogs and the other stole the feed, they were still losing $5 a head.

376.   Farmer: Does your boyfriend have any money?
Daughter: You men are all alike. That's what he asked about you!

377.   One winter morning, the farmer heard his wife trying unsuccessfully to start her car. He went outside and asked, "Did you try choking it?" "No," she replied, gritting her teeth, "but I sure felt like it."

378.   In Texas, a rich farmer is one who has white wall tires on his manure spreader.

379.   "What are you building?" a tourist asked a farmer who was erecting a building. "Wal," the farmer answered, "if'n I can rent it, it's a rustic cottage, an' if'n I can't, it's a cowshed."

380.   The happy farmer prepares for plot luck. If it all works out, he celebrates by a few days fishing and refers to himself as a happy hooker.

381.   When a not-too-handsome young farmer proposed marriage, he said, "I know I'm not much to look at." The young lady replied, "That's all right. You'll be out in the field most of the time."

382.   Apparently the government publishes three kinds of information on Farmers Intentions: lies, dang lies, and statistics.

383.   A farmer in Las Vegas got so excited at hitting the jackpot that he poured a beer in the slot machine and drank a cup of nickels.

RX for That Ailing Speech

RX #23. Farming has always been a good source of material. It is a well-known fact that making a living from the soil is a risky proposition and few people are willing to accept such a rigorous life. It has become popular in recent years, however, for numerous speakers to refer to themselves as "good old country boys." This is a mistake in most instances unless the speaker really and truly is a "good old country boy" and has some kind of credentials to back up his contention. The other way to use material of this nature is to simply tell it on your father, your country cousin, a grandfather, etc. Quoting your grandfather is an especially effective way of handling material concerning farmers and their satirical view of city slickers, government, foreign policy, and a host of other situations which lend themselves to the use of farm-type jokes, quips and stories.

* * * * * *

384. A local chicken farmer thought he had a miracle ingredient for feed. He was adding gunpowder to the laying mash. A fox got into the hen house and several of the stronger girls flew into the downtown district and exploded. Nobody was hurt but 6 people were overcome by feathers.

385. A farm wife was asked how long they were going to be on vacation. "Forty-two meals," she replied.

386. Farmer, carrying a small pig under one arm at the country fair meets friend. "Did you win that at the fair?" "I certainly did," the little pig says.

387. A farmer and his wife, married happily for almost half a century, were sitting in the front porch swing in the cool of the evening. The sun was going down in a blaze of color, the birds were trilling their evening song, the soft breeze wafted the scent of honeysuckle across the porch. The moment was a moving one. The farmer felt strangely, moved to speech, and blurted out, "Martha, sometimes I love you so much I can hardly keep from telling you."

388. The local cattle raiser sold his beef herd at a loss and went to his banker with the tale of woe. "I've got some bad news for you and some good news," he told the loan arranger. "The bad news is that I marketed my beef at a loss and I can't pay the overdue notes you are holding. The rancher added, "The good news is that I'm staying with you."

389. "Farm products cost more than they used to," the city dweller remarked, somewhat surprised. "Yes," replied the farmer. "When a farmer is supposed to know

the botanical name of what he's raisin', and the ento-
mological name of the insect that eats it, and the
pharmaceutical name of the chemical that will kill it,
somebody's got to pay."

590

FASHION

390. Two girls were looking at the latest fashion
photos. "Long dresses are out, they pick up germs."
"Yeah, besides, I like what short dresses pick up."

391. Long skirts are like prohibition. The joints are
still there but they're harder to spot.

392. Platform shoes keep young girls off the streets.
Way off the streets!

393. I tried to grow a beard, but it didn't turn out too
well. People kept saying clever things like, "Is that a
beard you're wearing or are you holding your head
under your arm?"

394. If women dress for other women, as so many
observers claim, it's certainly difficult to explain their
appearance at the supermarket.

395. Watch fashion pages and you'll learn that the
beach this summer is going to be a place where a man
will look his best—at the girls. And he'll only have to
look half as long ... to see twice as much.

396. Fashions really give you a whole new look. Last
Saturday night, we were going out so my wife put on her
high heel shoes, a wig, blue eye shadow, false eye lashes,
silver lipstick. Then she went into the kid's room and
said, "Now drink your milk, go to bed at nine, and I don't
want to hear a peep out of you from the babysitter." She

blew them a kiss and departed. One kid turned to the other and said, "Who was that?"

397.   The way women dress on the beaches, you would think they'd lost faith in men's imagination.

398.   Fashion note: There will be no change in men's pockets this year.

369, 730, 786

FATHERS

399.   A father is a fellow who has pictures where his money used to be.

400.   A young boy, during an argument with his parents, cried, "I want excitement, adventure, money and beautiful women. I'll never find it here at home, so I'm leaving. Don't try to stop me." With that, he headed for the door. His father rose and followed close behind. The boy said, "Didn't you hear what I said? Don't try to stop me." "Who's trying to stop you?" replied his father. "If you wait a minute, I'll go with you."

401.   My father is one who remembers when a family was considered shiftless if they lived from payday to payday. Now they are considered above average.

402.   "Ma, am I descended from the apes?"
      "I don't know—I never met your father's side of
         the family."

403.   Father to small son dragging the top half of a bikini bathing suit along the beach: "Now show Daddy exactly where you found it."

267, 270, 373, 403, 449, 544, 551, 552, 555, 644, 1041, 1157

RX for That Ailing Speech

RX #24. Note that entry 403 depicts a beach, a small boy, a bikini and a father. This is almost a cartoon, and, in fact, would make a good cartoon. Some stories such as this might be better explained to the audience if you actually made it a cartoon in their mind. The line might then be delivered in this way so that people immediately begin to see the situation developing, not in real life, but in cartoon from which they expect to be humorous: I saw a cartoon the other day in the local paper. A small boy was dragging the top half of a bikini bathing suit along the beach and his father was walking along with him, leaning over to say something. The caption on the cartoon read: "Now show daddy exactly where you found it."

Many stories lend themselves to the use of the cartoon image. It is an old trick that many professional humorists use, although sparingly, to get the maximum mileage from a line that lends itself to the proper interpretation. Some speakers, who use visual aids may even have an artist draw a cartoon, show it to the audience and deliver the caption verbally. If you doubt the effectiveness of this technique think about the Tonight Show. Notice how Johnny Carson shows still photos from old movies and fills in the plot with a punch line?

267, 270, 373, 403, 449, 544, 551, 552, 555, 644, 1041, 1157

FIRE DEPARTMENT

404. "Did the hotel burn down 'cause the fire department didn't make it soon enough?" "No, they couldn't get the hose through the revolving door."

405. A man phoned the local fire station one night and asked, "Is this the Fire Department?" "Yes," he was told.

"Listen," said the man. "I've just moved here, and I've spent a lot on the garden. I engaged men to..." "Where's the fire?" interrupted the officer at the station. "...dig out the old stuff and lay out new lawns and beds. The lawn alone set me back..." "Is your house on fire?" yelled the officer. "No," the man said, "but the one next door is, and if anybody gets in touch with you about it, I don't want clodhoppin' firemen draggin' hoses all over my new garden, see?"

406.   A woman called the fire department and said, "Come quick! My house is on fire!" "How do we get there?" the dispatcher asked. After a short pause she replied, "Don't you still have your little red truck?"

632, 790

FISHING

407.   An Alaskan was asked why he quit guiding hunters and now was a fishing guide. "Well, nobody has mistaken me for a fish yet," he said.

408.   A fellow claims he was fishing from a boat over a man-made reef on a coastal bay. He thought he had hooked an old car body. His skin diving buddy told him he probably had a huge redfish and he would go down and shoot him with his spear gun. After 15 minutes, he surfaced, out of oxygen and ammunition. Exhausted, he gasped, "Every time I get a clear shot at him, he rolls up the window."

409.   It got so dry one year that we were catching catfish that had ticks.

410.   Two fellows were fishing from a dock when an alligator nipped one of them on the foot. The fisherman screamed, "An alligator just bit off one of my toes!" "Which one?" his buddy asked. "How do I know!" the wounded angler said in disgust. "All alligators look alike to me."

411. Sunday school teacher: "Do you suppose Noah did a lot of fishing?"
Six-year-old: "What? With only two worms?"

412. Two sportsmen, in quest of new fishing grounds, turned down a dirt road with a "Closed" sign blocking it. They chose to drive around the sign for three laborious miles only to find the road was a dead end. With great difficulty they turned the car around and drove silently back to the sign where they noted this inscription scrawled on the back of the road sign: "When the hell are you gonna believe us?"

413. A young wife, hoping to divert her husband's fanatic interest in fishing to romance, surprised him on his birthday with a fantastic waterbed. He had it stocked with trout.

414. It's always the big ones that get away. That's because a fisherman's eyes are bigger than his hooks.

380, 1003

FRIENDS

415. We are close friends. He has been over to our house ... not when we were there, of course.

416. My friend bought life insurance and improved his wife's housekeeping at the same time—now she's even waxing the tub.

417. Randy Cline, secretary of the West Virginia Press Association, claims that when he first decided to run for the House of Delegates, his brother was his campaign manager. "Hey," said the brother, "I got a great idea. It'll get you a lot of publicity, even national publicity. What I'll do, if you've got no objections, is I'll get 1,500 of your friends to put up a penny apiece and that's how we'll get the money to pay your filing fee." Randy agreed the scheme was a good one and his brother left to hop to it. A short time later, he was back. "Listen," he said. "Let's modify the idea a little bit. It might not get you any national publicity but you're not running for national office anyway. Let's get 150 friends to put up a dime apiece for the filing fee." Fine, fine, said Randy and his brother returned to the task. Not too much time had passed before the brother looking somewhat dispirited returned again. "Hey," he said. "I'll tell you, let's get 15 of your friends to put up a dollar and pay the filing fee that way." Okay, said Randy. About an hour later, his brother was back. "Listen," he said to Randy, "You got $7.50 on you?"

RX for That Ailing Speech

RX #25.   Note that the term "friend" can be applied to virtually every subject under the sun. If you are searching for material, this would be a good category that could be converted to use in virtually any situation. For example, the entries under "Fire Department" are very slim in this handbook but most of the material under some other category, such as "friends," could be used very effectively. Because it is a well-known fact that firemen live with dangerous situations, entry 416 could easily be converted to read, "The local fire chief has lived with danger all his life. He recently bought a big life insurance policy and remarked that if he had known it would have made his wife a better housekeeper, he would have bought it long ago. Now she's even waxing the bath tub."

The term "friend" is also a good one to use whenever you want to use the wit and wisdom of an anonymous person. This allows you to quote another source so that, if the material does not go well, you can merely shrug it off as bad advice. If it does go well, in the minds of the audience, you are a clever person for having spotted the wit and for having reported it.

418. A pessimist read his horoscope which said, "Make new friends and see what happens." He made three new friends and nothing happened. Now he complains that he's stuck with three new friends.

419. I have a friend who really knows how to handle Las Vegas. He left here in a $7,000 Cadillac and returned on a $75,000 bus.

420. My friend, Mike, said to me, "I just can't stand hippies." Just then a hippy organ grinder and his monkey came by and Mike pitched the monkey a quarter. "Why'd you do that?" I asked. "I thought you couldn't stand hippies." "Yeah," said Mike, "but they're so cute when they're little."

421. I have a friend who is a true gentleman. He is one who knows how to play the bagpipe, but doesn't.

422. I have another friend, Fred, who decided to sell his house, and realized that, before he could sell it, he'd have to clean out his garage. Everybody tried to get him to throw this away and that away. "No, I'm going to need this..." Fred would reply. "No, that's too good to throw away..." So he rented a miniwarehouse and moved all the stuff from the garage into it. He secured it with a special magnet-type lock. But that wasn't secure enough. Burglars broke into it. "But what really hurt," says Fred, "was that they didn't even take anything."

423. I have a friend who is so shy he won't undress in front of a princess phone.

424. A philosophic friend says every man is a damn fool for at least five minutes every day; wisdom consists of not exceeding this limit.

425. All this confusion about leaded and unleaded gasoline and octane ratings brings to mind the story of the fellow who claimed he could taste any liquid and tell the brand, place of origin and the year of vintage. His friends put him to the test. Blindfolded, he faced a battery of glasses which held an assortment of beverages. He scored well until he tasted from a glass of gasoline which a joker had slipped in. The tester grimaced, spat and shouted, "That's gasoline?" "We know," said the joker, "but what octane?"

426.   Tell your friend a falsehood and if he keeps it a secret, tell him the truth.

427.   "Roots" got a friend of mine interested in his family tree, too. He paid a research company $1,000 to check on his geneology and then another $500 to forget what they found.

428.   Tough guys have always been around. Back on Vinegar Hill where I grew up some friends were so tough they thought King Kong was effeminate.

429.   I have a friend who doesn't smoke, drink, stay up late or flirt with the girls. In short, he's everything I don't ever want to be.

RX for That Ailing Speech

RX #26.   Entry 429 is another good case for acting out a piece of wit to receive maximum stimulation of the minds in the audience. When delivering a line like this, the first sentence can be played on the "square." The punch line can be delivered much more effectively if when you get to the point where you say "he's everything I don't ever want to be," you visably, exaggeratingly shake your head and shudder when you get to the phrase "ever want to be." This is called selling a story with body language.

*   *   *   *   *   *

430.   My friend invented a new way to beat the gambling tables in Las Vegas: When you get off the plane, walk into the propeller.

431.   My deep-sea diver friend had scarcely gotten down to the bottom when a message came from the surface which left him in a dilemma. "Come up quick," he was told. "The ship is sinking."

432. I have a friend who grew up poor; claims things haven't changed all that much: "I'm too poverty-stricken to afford a shower or bathtub. On Saturday nights, I just streak through a car wash."

433. A friend who visited Mud Flats, Wyoming said it's a quiet place: "I bought a book entitled, WHAT TO DO IN MUD FLATS AT NIGHT. I turned the first page and it said, 'You're doing it.'"

30, 88, 91, 320, 324, 328, 439, 507, 611, 621, 659, 1152, 1207, 1214

GOSSIP

434. A gossip is a person who puts two and two together even when they're not.

435. There isn't as much harm in things going in one ear and out the other as there is in it passing through a lame brain and a loose tongue.

436. A few employees were talking about the office tongue-wag the other day. "I'm not saying where he tends to put his foot," one of them said, "but I understand he suffers from athlete's mouth."

GRAY HAIR

437. Nothing makes gray hair look more attractive than being bald.

438. Gray hair is worthless if the brain is still green.

439. Perhaps the best thing for gray hair is having bald-headed friends.

213

GOVERNMENT

440.   A sure way to keep crime from paying is to let the government run it.

441.   The more bureaus Washington has, the more we stand to lose our drawers.

442.   "I'm selling tickets to a dinner honoring our former governor. There will be door prizes, and the tickets are only $10 each," said a fund raiser. "I'd rather knock his teeth down his throat," replied an irate taxpayer. "That's the first prize!" said the salesman.

443.   There is a rumor that Adolf Hitler still lives and serves as an economic adviser in Washington.

444.   The government is my shepherd, I need not work. It alloweth me to lie down on a good job, it leadeth me beside still factories; it destroyeth my initiative. It leadeth me in the path of a parasite for politics' sake, yea, though I walk through the valley of laziness and deficit spending, I will feel no evil, for the government is with me. It prepareth an economic Utopia for me by appropriating the earnings of my grandchildren. It filleth my head with false security. Surely the government should care for me all the days of my life and I shall dwell in a fool's paradise forever.

445.   Grand Canyon guide: "It took millions of years to carve out this."
    Tourist: "Oh, was it a government project?"

446.   The Federal government publishes pamphlets telling how you fix just about anything so it will run right—except, maybe, the Federal government.

RX for That Ailing Speech

RX #27.   The government is always an excellent source for ribbing. It is generally best to rib the Federal government if material such as this is being used at a local government meeting. It is quite appropriate to reverse the procedure if the situation involves a number of dignitaries from the Federal government. In other instances, if your listeners happen to be a mixture of local and Federal authorities, there is little danger in alienating anyone through the good natured kidding of all those involved under the general category of government. Humor such as this is universally accepted. Even in countries which are communistic or where they have ruthless dictators, the people joke about the ruthlessness of the governing power.

Will Rogers was perhaps one of the keenest, most successful, political observers of all time. He was able to burst the bubble of pomp and ceremony with his sharp barbs. That allowed people and politicians to laugh at the inadequacy of the system. One of the strengths of our form of government is the fact that we realize it has many weaknesses. Government is always a sure-fire source of some humor in almost every meeting around this country. Just think of the stories that involve the President, the President's brother, mother, children, sister, relatives, friends, etc. This area is always fair game for the humorist and it is open season all year long.

* * * * * *

447. Where but in the U.S. could you watch an American historical documentary made by the BBC on a TV set manufactured in Japan?

448. A hotel clerk asked a registering guest what kind of view he preferred, and the guest responded:: "One overlooking the bill."

449. Government bureaus often come across unique evasions on the forms applicants fill in. One man, in the space asking the cause of parental death, wrote: "Father was taking part in a public function, and the platform gave way, ending his life." Subsequent investigations disclosed that his father had been hanged for cattle rustling.

450.   With the botched-up job the government is doing, we can all be thankful we ain't getting our money's worth.

451.   One man asked another: "What is your brother doing?"
The other man replied: "Nothing."
"But I thought he was trying to get a government job?"
"He got it."

452.   Government is a 50-50 proposition. They tell us what to do and we tell them where to go.

453.   The government says it's okay to get drunk on alcohol, high on marijuana, and emphysemic on cigarettes. But, friend, don't ever try to get sweet on saccharin.

104, 382, 1133

HOME

454.   Home is where parents wait for their turn at the family car.

455.   Legally, the man is head of the house, and a pedestrian has the right of way. Both are fairly safe, until they exercise those rights.

456.   Maybe it's just a coincidence but ever since women began carrying purses, more and more homes are being built without attics.

457.   Home is the place where a man can say anything he pleases—no one there listens to him anyway.

310, 628, 1090, 1189, 1235

HOSPITALS

458.   Then there was the hospital patient complaining about the cost of some minor surgery. "What this country needs," he griped, "is a good $50 scar."

459.   After a patient underwent an operation at the local hospital and came out of the anesthesia, he asked a nurse: "How come all the shades on the windows are pulled down?" The nurse answered: "The house across the street is on fire, and we didn't want you to wake up thinking that the operation was a failure."

460.   Statistics disclose that babies are born to every fifth person going into the hospital. If you've already been in four times, be prepared.

461.   While in the hospital, *Seattle Times'* columnist Walt Evans received many get-well cards. Among them: "I talked to your doctor and frankly, he's very upset ... you've got to stop asking him to kiss it and make it well!" "You must be feeling better. The nurses have put a little sign on your door: DANGER, man recovering."

463, 1185

RX for That Ailing Speech

RX #28.   Following the line of reasoning previously described as the "Laugh-In Theory," stories like the ones listed under the heading of "Hospitals" are devoid of everything but the punch line. It is important to remember that a line used to hopefully elicit laughter must be carefully placed so that it is delivered during the time when the mind is most receptive to the thought process being developed.

For this reason, it is important on many occasions to precede lines such as these with some introductory remarks to "set up" the audience for the line. An example of this follows. "I've been healthy as a horse my whole life, but the other day I had to visit a friend in the hospital. I was passing by the maternity ward and couldn't help but notice all the cute new babies being displayed behind the glass. I struck up a conversation with a doctor there and discovered some very startling information about hospitals. Statistics disclose that babies are born to every fifth person going into the hospital. So, take warning, if you have already been in four times, be prepared."

Visualize your own "set ups" and you will soon have pieces of material that are uniquely your own.

HUSBANDS

462. Any husband who can forget his mistakes is probably married to a woman with a poor memory.

463. The phone rang in the maternity ward and an excited voice on the other end said: "This is George Smith and I'm bringing my wife in—she's about to have a baby!" "Calm down," replied the attendant. "Tell me, is this her first baby?" "No," the voice replied, "this is her husband."

464. It's a smart husband who puts his foot down only to shift his position.

465. A lady was two hours late getting home and her angered husband yelled, "Where have you been?" "At the beauty parlor," snapped back his wife. "Too bad," yelled the angry husband, "that you didn't get waited on."

466. The reason many husbands never speak out of turn is they don't have one.

467. A woman used to put her husband's lunch in the refrigerator every night. He gets up so early in the morning that half the time he forgets it. Every night now she puts his car keys in the bag with the lunch.

468. A middle-aged lady says her husband always puts off his Christmas shopping until the very last minute—usually Christmas Eve—and then he runs out and grabs whatever comes within reach. When she opened one of her gifts from him, she discovered a beautiful dress. "It's lovely," she exlaimed. "Aboslutely lovely." Then she took a closer look while her husband preened and congratulated himself on his selection. "I saw it in the store window," he said, "and I knew it was for you." "There is one little thing," the lady said. "What's that?" her husband wanted to know. "Well," said his wife, "I haven't been pregnant for 20 years."

469. My husband went all out this year. He bought $5,000 worth of furniture on the lay awake plan.

470. The tired husband dragged himself through his front door and dropped wearily into a chair. His wife asked: "Busy day at the office, dear?" He sighed: "Terrible. The computer broke down in the middle of the morning and we all had to think."

471. You know we're in a recession when Zsa Zsa Gabor hangs on to a husband for more than a year.

472. Young wife in newly purchased texturized pantyhose: "Well, what do you think?" Husband: "Leave it alone. If it doesn't clear up in a couple of days, then you'd better see the doctor."

473. "What is your husband getting out of jogging down the road?"
"Tired and overheated."

474. "You look tired."
"I am. I've been all over town trying to get something for my husband."
"Had any offers?"

475. The company president was described by his wife: "My husband is nobody's fool. He's self-employed."

476.   Husband: "Can you guess where I've been?"
Wife: "Yes, but let's hear your story first."

477.   "How can you treat me like that after I gave you the best years of my life?" the wife said. "Good grief!" shouted her husband, "those were your best?"

478.   HENNY YOUNGMAN: "I've cut down—my wife wanted a foreign car—and I bought her a ricksha. My wife just had plastic surgery—I cut up all her credit cards. I bought her a mink outfit—a rifle and trap."

17, 90, 283, 284, 286, 387, 413, 567, 634, 647, 950, 1164, 1223

RX for That Ailing Speech

RX #29.   Note that throughout this handbook, certain well-known comedians are quoted. Henny Youngman (entry 478) is well known for his delivery of short mini-stories. If you have ever heard Henny Youngman, you will recognize his style immediately once you hear it again. It is quick, pointed and rapid-fire. The best way to use material that is a part of another person's style is to give them the courtesy of quoting their material. Not only are you using the material in an ethical manner, but you also allow the mind of the audience to imagine the style and personality of the person displaying this form of wit.

You should be cautioned, however, not to base your whole presentation on someone else's material and/or style of delivery. It is very easy to overdo a good thing. But, numerous, well-known personalities can be utilized in dealing with humor. Personalities with certain quirks or peculiar mannerisms are especially well adapted for imitation and delivery. Just think of Rodney Dangerfield and you conjure up the image of a man straightening his tie, with a frenzied look saying, "I don't get no respect." Jack Benny brings to mind the long stare with the hand on the side of the face. W. C. Fields brings to mind a certain voice inflection that is easy for most people to imitate. If you imitate these personalities very, very sparingly, you can lend a great deal to the entertainment value of your remarks.

17, 90, 283, 284, 286, 387, 413, 567, 634, 950, 1164, 1223

IRS

479.   The guy next door got back from the Internal Revenue office and he says he's all paid up to 1956.

480.   Untold wealth: That's the kind the IRS is interested in.

481.   Walking along a street in Cleveland, a man was attracted by frightening screams from a house. He ran in to investigate and found a frantic mother whose small boy had swallowed a quarter. Seizing the child by the heels, he held him up, gave him a few shakes, and the coin dropped to the floor. The grateful mother was lost in admiration. "You certainly knew how to get it out of him." she marveled. "Are you a doctor?" "No, madam," replied the stranger, "I'm with the IRS."

482.   Millionaire: "I want to be cremated and my ashes sent to the IRS with a note 'Now you have it all, you dirty...'"

483.   Cheating on the IRS is one small step toward balanced papers, one giant leap toward the pen.

558, 686, 995, 1135

INDIANS

484.   After taking several snapshots of an elderly Indian chief, the vacationer asked, "Have you lived on the reservation all your life?" "Not yet," retorted the chief.

485.   One day the Lone Ranger and Tonto rode to the top of a hill overlooking the plains. Peering around, the masked man said suddenly, "Tonto, there's a war party of Indians approaching from the south." "We go north, Kemo sabe," said Tonto. The Lone Ranger then said, "Oh, my God, Tonto. There are Indians coming from the east. And another war party coming from the west. What are we going to do?" As Tonto rode off, he called back over his shoulder, "What do you mean we, white man?"

486.   A man returns from the North Woods with word that the Indians are predicting a severe winter. The prediction is based on the size of the white man's wood piles.

487.   The Indians brewed a potent booze that was called "The Blast of the Mohicans."

488.   Historians recently unearthed the very first treaty between white men and the Indians. It says the red man can keep his lands for as long as the river runs, the sun rises and the grass grows—or 90 days, whichever comes first.

489.   As the dark-skinned young man came out of the receiving room at the Red Cross Blood Center, a lady in the waiting room asked, "Are you a full-blooded Indian?" "No, lady," replied the Cherokee. "Right now I'm a pint short."

490.   The Indian squaw was explaining the facts of life to her young daughter. "Stork not bring papoose. It sometimes come by beau and error."

RX for That Ailing Speech

RX #30.   Here's a point to keep in mind. Some things that will appear funny on a written page will not translate as well to the spoken form unless great care is taken in setting up the story so that the listener can quickly grasp the play on words. I refer especially to joke 490 concerning the Indian squaw. The play on words here concerns "beau" and "error" as related in sound to bow and arrow. If you use this story without any setup, most of the audience probably will not catch it.

The way to use this is to introduce the story with something like, "On the reservations out in Arizona, Indian mothers just like whites are concerned about their daughters. Indian maidens are attracted to the same kind of beau, the kind that is six feet tall and drops around the teepee for a look see. No matter the race, every girl has her beau and every mother is concerned about that. It's like the Indian squaw who explained the facts of life to her young daughter: 'Stork not bring papoose. It sometimes come by beau and error.'"

Don't make the mistake of explaining so much that the element of surprise is lost. The mind loves a puzzle quickly grasped but concealed until the punch line releases the key to putting the picture together. By leaving out the last part, the mind is deceived into believing that it figured out the whole puzzle by itself with lightning rapidity.

INFLATION

491. Inflation is when you buy ink, paper, a printing press, run off millions and lose money on the deal.

492. It's inflation when you pay $5 for the $2 haircut you used to get for $1 when you had hair.

493. Inflation's getting so bad that even people who weren't going to buy anything are complaining about prices.

494. Inflation hasn't ruined everything. A dime can still be used as a screwdriver.

495. "Inflation," says one local wit, "means being broke with a lot of money in your pocket."

496.   Even with inflation, two can still live as cheap as one—but only half as long.

497.   The best way to beat inflation is to join a new organization called Customers Anonymous. Whenever you think about buying something, you phone someone in the group and he comes over and talks you out of it.

498.   Inflation is when, after you finally get the money to buy something, it isn't enough.

499.   The President isn't ending inflation, so we must learn to live with it. The first thing we need is a 25-hour work-week so that we can have three jobs instead of just two.

500.   The best way to slow down inflation is to send it through the mail.

501.   Seen in a Nebraska cafe: "Due to inflation, we've been forced to increase all prices immediately. Water will be twice as free."

502.   One company refuses to worry: "The balloon industry has lived with inflation for years."

INSECTS

503.   A most happy experience for ladybugs is to discover that not all ladybugs are ladies. It's also true that some mailmen are women.

504.   People who tell you never to let little things bother you have never tried sleeping in a room with a mosquito.

505.   I wonderingly asked: "Do mosquitoes go to the bathroom?" And my wife said, "Sure, I saw six of them in there this morning."

506. "Have you had this place exterminated?"
"No, we stamped out the need with a troupe of Spanish Flemenco Dancers."

507. My friend talked me into going camping. There must be a correlation between being a camper and being a masochist. Why else would you put a 50-pound sack on your back and walk until you get blisters on your feet? We camped in a place called Mosquito Creek. One mosquito was so big he showed up on radar. Not only did he bite me and suck my blood, he left footprints on my arm.

RX for That Ailing Speech

RX #31. Here is a point that is often forgotten by the lay speaker. The use of a few props may enliven a story and give it a special visual twist that will bring out the humor. Take the story about mosquitos (entry 507). This could be used in a slide presentation for almost any outdoor association. Use a few "staged" photographs and mix them in with your regular presentation. Take a photograph of someone cracking a whip, a close-up of bandaged feet and a shot of some tiny human footprint marks on an arm.

Imagine the chuckles when you recite the following, complete with photographs: "There must be a correlation between being a camper and being a masochist (photo of a whip cracker). Why else would you put a 50-pound sack on your back and walk until you get blisters on your feet (close-up of camper rubbing tired feet). One mosquito was so big he showed up on radar. Not only did he bite me and suck my blood, he left footprints on my arm (close-up of arm with tiny footprints)." Get the picture? Your audience can't miss it.

* * * * * *

508. A bee has to visit 2,000 blossoms in order to make one tablespoon of honey. Fortunately, they have nothing else to do.

509.   Do you know what you call an insect that leaps over fourteen cans of bug spray? Weevile Knievel.

510.   Waterbeds are so popular, I saw some bedbugs taking swimming lessons.

511.   Two flies landed on a knife handle that lay atop some round, sliced cold cuts. After eating a good portion of meat, the flies flew away and immediately dropped dead. The moral: Don't fly off the handle when you're full of baloney.

512.   Daisy June: "Listen to them June bugs all snuggled down cozy in the grass, chirping away. Clem, why can't we do something like that?"
Clem's response: "Shucks, Daisy June, I can't rub my hind legs together to chirp like that."

INSURANCE

513.   He had his car insured against fire and they tried to sell him some theft coverage, too. "That would be a waste of money," he said. "Who's going to steal a burning car?"

514.   He won't buy life insurance because he says it would be just his luck to die anyway.

515.   A fellow's barn burned. His insurance man said, "We'll pay off. Give you another one just like you had." "In that case, you can cancel the insurance on my wife."

516.   To insurance man: "What would I get if this building burned down tonight?" ... "About ten years."

517.   Fun is like insurance—the older you get the more it costs.

518.   The insurance agent across the hall says cosmetic surgeons can do such wonderful things these days he feels he's missing something by being handsome already.

JOBS

519. A couple of fellows were discussing their boss. One said: "On the outside he's lowdown and ornery. Underneath though, he's just the opposite—ornery and lowdown."

520. The neighbor's boy got a steady job—changing the gasoline price signs at service stations.

521. He takes it easy during regular working hours so that if there's any overtime, there'll be somebody fresh enough to do it.

522. "How long you been working here?"
"Since the boss threatened to fire me."

523. Finagle's Law: Once a job is fouled up, anything done to improve it makes it worse.

524. "This machine will do half your job for you."
"Good. Gimme two!"

525. He does the job of three men—Harpo, Chico and Groucho.

526. College grads are finding it difficult to get jobs. Whatever happened to the eleventh commandment, "Go forth and marry the boss' daughter"?

RX for That Ailing Speech

RX #32. Entry 526 is particularly appropriate for a young man who may have the chore of serving as spokesman for the annual company gathering. The story can be used in at least two ways, perhaps many more. If the young man has just graduated from college, the joke is on him because the audience will recognize the fact that he is putting himself down for having spent all those years in education when he could have used his head and sought the company of female companionship that had corporate backing. If the boss' daughter has truly just recently married, then the audience will accept the joke as being a good-natured slap at the boss' new son-in-law. In either case, the story would look like an ad-lib and the audience will be more receptive to it because they recognize the "inside" humor. A clever speaker looks for material that will appear to have an "inside" structure.

* * * * * *

527.   Seems these three Irishmen applied for work on a North Sea oil rig. All were qualified roughnecks and were offered contracts. The first Irishman signed his with an X. "And what's that?" the personnel manager asked. "Sure, and it's me name, Mike," said the Irishman. The second Irishman signed his contract XX. "Me full name, Pat Rafferty," he said. The third Irishman signed with a grand flourish—XXX. "Sean Kelly," he said,, "Ph.D., University of Dublin..."

528.   While we are earning our living by the sweat of our brow, some smart cookies are selling us sweat bands, cold drinks and air conditioning.

529.   The dimwit's first day at work, the employment manager told him: "It looks to me as if you've been fired from every job you ever had." "Well," he bragged, "you've got to admit I'm no quitter."

530.   A lot of fellows nowadays have a BA, MA, MD, or Ph.D. Unfortunately, they don't have a J-O-B.

531.   The time will soon be here when two million graduates leave college to look for positions—and wind up getting jobs.

532. A handyman looking for jobs ran this ad in a newspaper: "I can fix anything your husband can. And I'll do it now."

533. An out-of-work piano tuner made a fortune out in West Texas tightening barbwire fences.

534. After 20 years on the job, Max has finally reached a point in his life when he can take a two-hour lunch. Now his stomach can only take milk and crackers.

329, 450, 451, 499, 740

KIDS

535. The nice part about the way kids look today—for the first five to six years, if the father wanted a boy and the mother wanted a girl, both are satisfied.

536. Mother to son: "What have you learned about famous people in history?"
Son: "Not much, nobody lives more than two pages."

537. "Why did you kick your little brother in the stomach?"
"Cause he wouldn't turn around."

538. Kids may be deductible, but they're still taxing.

539. The teacher asked a fifth grader to name five things that contained milk. The kid wrote, "Butter, cream, cheese, and two cows."

540. There's the guy who cured his kid of tardiness. Bought him a car—now he goes to school early so he can find a parking place.

541.   The kid down the block is pretty tough. He plays Frisbee with manhole covers.

RX for That Ailing Speech

RX #33.   Kids are a great subject for humor because everyone can relate to them, either as having once been a child, or as they observed some of their own. The process keeps repeating itself as parents also become grandparents so that the subject of kids never runs out of style. Also with a simple twist, all of this material can be utilized on grown-ups. Just imagine how each of the adults in your audience may have acted as children and you have a built-in bridge to humor. For instance, the purchasing manager of a company is usually considered heartless: "Imagine our purchasing manager as a kid. He was pretty tough. He played Frisbee with manhole covers." The audience gets a double image, not only of a tough guy but of a mean little kid.

*   *   *   *   *   *

542.   Raising kids—you spend half your time instilling them with knowledge and the other half trying to get them not to be so darn smart.

543.   Nothing discourages parenthood more than driving a school bus.

544.   One teenage kid to another: "Hey, you had your long hair cut off. How much weight did you lose?" Second kid: "About 200 pounds—I got my father off my back."

545.   A young entrepreneur explained how he did it: "I gave a dozen white mice to all the neighborhood kids—free. I charged their parents a fee for taking them back."

546.   A welfare receiver with ten kids was told that he couldn't keep having kids and receiving money. "I'll put a stop to it. If I have any more, I'll hang myself," he said.

One year later, number eleven arrived. When reminded of his promise he said, "I started to do it; had the rope over a barn rafter when it occurred to me I might be hanging the wrong man."

547. I always wanted to go to Europe in the worst possible way. Last year I did—with the kids.

548. A traveling orator, after his speech, was approached by a woman dragging a small boy. "Oh, Professor," she wailed, "I'm just filled with your message." Looking down at the small fry, the lecturer inquired, "How about you, sonny?" "Yeh," said the boy. "I got a belly full, too."

549. RODNEY DANGERFIELD: "My kid drives me nuts. For three years now he goes to a private school. He won't tell me where it is."

550. A kindergarten teacher was glad to see Friday roll around. She was testing the kiddies' powers of observation: "How many eyes does a cat have?" "Two!" "How many ears does a cat have?" "Two!" "How many tails does a cat have?" Voice from back row: "Good grief! Ain't you ever seen a cat?"

551. "My kid is so spoiled," said one disgruntled father to another, "that the only way I can punish him is to take away his grandmother."

552. Man sitting on his front porch at 3 a.m.
Cop: "What are you doing here?"
Man: "I forgot my key and I'm waiting for my kids to come home and let me in the house."

553. Someday the neighborhood kids are going to go too far. And when they do, let's hope they stay there.

554. At show and tell, a kid discussed his visit to the zoo. "Teacher, I saw a Hip...Hipa...Hopi..." "Hippopatamus?" asked the teacher. "I don't know what you call it, but it looked like 9,000 pounds of liver," the kid replied.

555.   In an argument between two boys about what their fathers were able to do, Joey asked, "You know the Atlantic Ocean? Well, my dad dug the hole for it!" Ronnie replied, "That's nothing. You know the Dead Sea? Well, my dad's the one who killed it!"

556.   The most disappointed kid I ever heard of was one who crawled under a tent to see a circus and it was a revival meeting.

RX for That Ailing Speech

RX #34.   This story (entry 556), although extremely short, can be utilized as a pro or con religious slap. If the line is used on someone in the audience, it will probably get a great deal of response if the individual is a known boozer or a slightly irreverent character. The story could also be used to jab a little good-natured fun in the direction of a lay preacher or someone in the hierarchy of the church, such as a bishop. The key to using stories such as this is to fit the story to a personality, even if it is your own, as a fun-loving means to laugh off human frailty.

* * * * * *

557.   A housewife on Elm Street says life would be a lot easier if we had permanent diapers and disposable kids.

558.   One youngster must know about income tax. He was heard saluting the colors with, "I pledge my allowance to the flag..."

559.   When a small boy came home one evening with $30 after selling magazine subscriptions, his father proudly asked: "How many customers did you have to go to in order to make all this money?" The boy explained: "I sold all the subscriptions to one man. His dog bit me."

560. Second grader: "My teacher asked me if I had any brothers or sisters."

Mother: How nice of her to take an interest in you."

Second grader: "Yes, and when I told her I was an only child, she said, 'thank goodness.'"

561. Studious kids were once called bookworms. Now that they're taught by TV tapes—do you call them tapeworms?

562. It was graduation day, and mom was trying to take a picture of her son in a cap and gown posed with his father. "Let's try to make this look natural," she said. "Junior, put your arm around your dad's shoulder." The father answered, "If you want it to look natural, why not have him put his hand in my pocket?"

563. The doctor had two children, and everyone said they were the prettiest girls in town. "Say," a visitor to the town said, "Who are those pretty little girls?" "They're the doctor's children," a boy said. "He always keeps the best for himself."

192, 193, 194, 221, 227, 396, 565, 807, 1051, 1114, 1146

KISSING

564. Kissing is a means of getting two people so close together that they can't see anything wrong with each other.

565. Two very, very young boys were discussing the girl problem. Said the first: "I've walked to school with her three times and carried her books. I bought her an ice cream soda twice. Now, do you think I ought to kiss her?" Replied his friend: "No, you don't need to. You've done enough for her already."

566. Kissing a girl is like getting olives out of a bottle. After the first one, the rest are easy.

567. Wife: "When Jones comes home, he kisses his wife on the porch. Why don't you do that?"
Husband: "Don't be silly, Ethyl, I hardly know the woman."

568. "Girls were harder to kiss in your day, weren't they, Grandpa?" the young man inquired. "Maybe so, but it wasn't so blamed dangerous," the grandfather answered. "I never heard of a sofa running off the road and smashing into a telephone pole."

569. "What would I have to give you for just one little kiss?"
"Chloroform."

570. Douglas Walkington, chemist for Canadian Industries, says that kissing is just chemistry, and is based on a craving for salt. "The caveman," he stated, "found that salt helped him stand the summer heat, and that he could get it by licking a companion's cheek. Also, he found that if the companion were of the opposite sex, the process became more interesting. "Then," Mr. Walkington concluded, "everybody forgot all about salt."

571. Nobody ever kissed a girl unexpectedly. The closest you can come to it is to kiss her sooner than she expected.

572. Mother (horrified): "Kissing a man you just met! You never saw me doing that!"
Daughter: "No, but I'll bet Grandma did."

573. A boy saw his date to the door and asked for "a real old-fashioned kiss." She called her grandmother.

574. Know what's the hardest thing in the world to do? Kiss a chicken on the lips.

575. Boy: If you contradict me once more, I'm gonna kiss you.

Girl: Oh, no you're not!

665, 862

RX for That Ailing Speech

RX #35. The subject of kissing is extremely versatile for a mixed audience of most any age. The reason is simple. It has a sexy connotation yet is completely clean and acceptable for discussion in public. So many comedians and speakers think they must get vulgar in order to get a rousing response from an audience, but here is one subject area that has extremely high interest among both sexes and yet has no taboos even among the most prudish listeners. In short, it is just clean fun of a high interest nature and you should take advantage of the subject area and obtain the maximum mileage from it. Here's another hint. A lot of the so called "dirty" jokes that strike your fancy can be converted, with the use of a little imagination, to an acceptable story that merely involves the act of kissing.

LANDLORDS

576. Our neighbor says his landlord asks too much for the rent. Last month he asked four times.

577. My landlord is such a hypocrite! He wrote a book on atheism and then prayed it would sell well.

578. My landlord said to practice courtesy. You never know when it might become popular again.

579. "One of my tenants told me recently that the couple living in the suite above him shouts and pounds on the floor until midnight nearly every evening," said a landlord. "When I asked him if he wanted to make a complaint, he said, 'Not really, I'm usually up practicing my trumpet until about that time anyway.'"

580.   Young lady: "How long would it take to walk to the police station from this apartment in case of an emergency?"

Landlord: "I really don't know. Nobody has ever made it before."

581.   A woman in a rooming house complained to the landlady that the man in the next room kept annoying her with indecent songs. "I am sure that you're mistaken," answered the landlady, "Mr. Brown never sings any songs." "I know," replied the woman, "but he whistles them."

582.   Landlord to new tenant: "You know we keep it very quiet and orderly here. Do you have children?" "No." "A piano, radio or TV?" "No." "Do you have a dog, cat, or parrot?" "No, the noisiest thing we ever had was a goldfish but we sold him because he snored."

LAWYERS

583.   Where there's a will, there's a probate lawyer.

584.   "Judge, I don't know what to do," the prisoner said. "Why, how's that?" the judge asked. The prisoner explained, "I swore to tell the truth, but every time I try, some lawyer objects."

585.   The "jury" is twelve people who decide which side has the best lawyers.

586.   Mike was on his deathbed and his soon-to-be widow, Bridget, called a lawyer to make Mike's will as she sat in on the important ceremonial.

"State your debts as quickly as possible," said the lawyer.

"Tim Reilly owes me $40," moaned Mike.

"Good," said the prospective widow.

"Ian O'Neill owes me $37," groaned Mike.

"Sensible to the last," replied his wife.

"To one Michael O'Callahan, I owe $200," said Mike.

"Blessed mother of God!" said his wife. "Hear the man rave!"

587.   A gift for the man who has everything: a lawyer to explain to the jury how he got everything!

588.   "Gentlemen of the jury," said the defense attorney, now beginning to warm to his summation. "The real question before you is, shall this beautiful young woman be forced to languish away her loveliest years in a dark prison cell? Or shall she be set free to return to her cozy little apartment at 4134 Seaside Street...there to spend her lonely, loveless hours in her boudoir, lying beside her little princess phone, 926-7873?"

589.   The difference between a lawyer and an attorney is that an attorney has a client.

590.   A young lawyer pleading his first case, had been retained by a farmer to prosecute a railroad for killing 24 hogs. He wanted to impress the jury with the magnitude of the injury. "Twenty-four hogs, gentlemen!" he cried. "Twenty-four! Twice as many as there are in the jury box."

279, 316, 1123

RX for That Ailing Speech

RX #36.   Lawyers are always a good subject for jokes because they are so visible in the U.S. One startling statistic is that America contains more lawyers than all of the rest of the world's countries combined. This has lead to high visibility and since they are involved with law enforcement, any type of scandal becomes ammunition for gags. One precaution in using lawyer jokes is to make sure that no lawyer in the audience is in trouble with the law. They will all recognize the sweet-sour truth in a humorous barb such as "My lawyer is the best in the business. He was asked to appear four times last week in District Court. All four times he was convicted." Note that by using the term "my lawyer," you have taken the pressure off of all other lawyers.

LIFE

591. Life gets tougher every day. Not only must we decide what things we don't do, but in what order we won't do them.

592. Most people die disappointed with life. They never saw what lay around the corner or over the hill, just what went down the drain.

593. All of us could live longer if we would give up those things that make us want to.

594. ALICE LONGFELLOW: "I have a simple philosophy for life...fill what's empty, empty what's full and scratch where it itches."

595. Instead of just biting the bullet, maybe we ought to try getting the lead out.

596. When life begins at 40, perhaps you've gotten your children married.

597. Life is divided into two very difficult parts— making a name for yourself, and then keeping it.

598. They say there are no signs of intelligent life on Mars. But I never heard of one of those rocks spending 12 billion dollars to fly down here.

599. One of the great disappointments in life is realizing you are a late bloomer only to discover you have no stalk on which to hang your blossom.

600.   Nothing makes it harder for two to live as cheaply as one as becoming three.

> **18, 19, 484, 714, 728, 827, 909, 916, 963, 1180**

RX for That Ailing Speech

RX #37. Humor can increase your creativity and be extremely helpful on jobs that require contact with people. It is a good tool for sales people, police, bank tellers and all other professions which deal with people. Suppose, for instance, that you are a bank teller. Imagine the giggles that might be produced when you lay in wait for a pregnant lady to approach your window. After having fulfilled her banking needs, rather than say, "Have a nice day," use the line above (600). She'll be pleased that you noticed and probably lead the laughter even if it's just between the two of you (or is it three?).

MAIL

601.   Know what you call a lady mailperson? A postal packing mama.

602.   Fearing that a rather bulky letter he had to mail might be overweight, the man had it checked at the post office. "Right on the nose," the clerk said, handing back the letter. The man put a stamp on the envelope and returned it to the clerk. "Whoops!" cried the clerk, tossing the letter on the scale again. "Now you're over!"

603.   One advantage of the new postage stamps is that when you write a girl a love letter, she'll know you mean it.

604.   The postal clerk said he didn't realize how slow the mail was until he got a picture postcard from Mt. Rushmore and there were only two faces on it.

605. Our postmaster has plans to speed up the mail service. He'll have a picture of himself on a stamp wearing his grin. He has such a big mouth, it'll be the first stamp in history that can lick itself.

606. How about that inscription on the mailman's tomb, "Returned to Sender."

607. Let us try to be grateful for practical things. Like be thankful the post office doesn't handle prayers.

608. Hear about the mailman who took his girlfriend to a motel and registered as Mr. and Mrs. Occupant?

609. If they keep upping postal rates, they may have to put a tranquilizer in the glue.

610. We can't stand another increase in the cost of postage. It already costs $1.10 to mail a letter from Seattle to Chicago—15 cents for the postage and 95 cents for the phone call to see if it got there.

611. I've got a friend taking a course from a correspondence school. Friday, the mailman told him he was going to be bussed to a different post office.

612. The postal service's credo, updated: "Neither snow nor rain, nor gloom of night stays their couriers from the swift completion of their appointed rounds—so there must be some other reason."

613. The postal rates are getting higher and higher. That confirms the rumor that the post office has been sold to the Arabs.

500

RX for That Ailing Speech

RX #38.   Imagine this. Among the greatest comedians of all time, Charlie Chaplin is listed near the top. Few people will disagree with this ranking. Yet, Charlie Chaplin gained his reputation without ever speaking a word. His humor was entirely pantomime. Yet, all his ideas had to come from some image, probably originally a verbal expression of a humorous event. Chaplin just used the reverse image procedure and developed the joke simply by sight.

This same principle can still be utilized through the use of physical humor—face and hands. The hands can be used to emphasize postal rates getting higher and higher, a frown can be used in conjunction with a term such as "meaner and meaner," a broad smile adds much to a term like "sexier and sexier." Used sparingly, physical humor can add much to some of your presentations that need a little help in visualization.

MARRIAGE

614.   Marriage can be very educational if a husband is willing to listen to all the lectures.

615.   A local spinster said she didn't need a husband. She had a stove that smoked, a parrot that cussed and a cat that stayed out all night. Then the phone rang and her response may have indicated a change of heart. "Will you marry me?" the voice asked. "Yes...who is this?"

616.   It's amazing how much little things can affect a marriage—like having a beautiful built-in kitchen and a gorgeous eat-out wife.

617.   An old fellow fell in love with a lady and got down on his knees and said there were two things he would like to ask her. She said, "Okay." He said, "Will you marry me?" She said, "Yes," then asked what his second question was. "Will you help me up?"

618.   The trouble with people who never forget is that they wind up married to people who never remember.

619.   Marriage is an institution. Marriage is love. Love is blind. Therefore, marriage is an institution for the blind.

620.   If marriages are made in heaven, how come so many get past quality control?

621.   A man said he didn't think people should get married on Sunday. "Why?" asked a friend. "Because," he said, "It ain't right to gamble on the Lord's Day."

622.   A new college course is being offered in the sex education field. It is called heterosexual premarital intradigitation...or...holding hands before marriage.

623.   Two young people from a commune wanted to get married. Both were dressed in U.S. Army surplus ponchos, thong sandals and had hair that looked like a brillo pad with a glandular condition. The minister couldn't even see their eyes. He couldn't distinguish between them so he just married them and said, "One of you may kiss the bride."

624.   He is so henpecked that when he gets sick, his wife chooses the illness.

625.   Husband: "I can't decide whether to go to a palmist or a mind reader."
Wife: "Go to the palmist. It's obvious you have a palm."

626.   A man who gives in when he is wrong is wise. A man who gives in when he's right is married.

627.   Don't be too sure he's a married man by the looks of him. He may be a bachelor with a headache.

628.   Melvin was celebrating his 50th wedding anniversary and explained his happy marriage: "At home I rule the roost—and my wife rules the rooster."

RX for That Ailing Speech

RX #39.   One reason so many people fail with humor is simply because they have no confidence in either themselves or the material they are using. Henny Youngman was once asked whom he admired most as a comedian. He named Milton Berle and was quoted as saying, "If I adopted anything from him, it was his way of doing things, his attitude—going out and being sure of yourself, believing in what you are doing." The point is that humor is so much attitude that it is difficult to separate the good material from the bad. Basically, if a story strikes you as being funny, your attitude will be such that you can convey the humor in it to an individual or an audience and they too will find it funny. Develop an attitude of confidence and use only material that you feel comfortably sure about.

*   *   *   *   *   *

629.   Husband to wife: "The doctor said tranquilizers would save our marriage. There's just one problem—how do we get your mother to take them?"

630.   A lady and her husband just returned from a trip to exotic places and a neighbor asked her how in the world they had been able to afford it. "We couldn't," the lady said. "But we discussed it and decided that when you got right down to it, we weren't able to afford just staying here at home either, and as long as we weren't going to be able to afford something, we might as well enjoy it while we were at it."

631.   Marriage for a woman these days is still the next best thing to having a man of her own.

632.   "My sister married a man in the fire department," a youth told a friend, who inquired, "Volunteer?" The youth replied, "Nope, Pa made him."

633.   Any man who thinks he's the boss of the house is probably married to a woman who knows how to keep a secret.

634.   A couple was watching a movie of Paul Newman in a torrid love story. When they left the theater, the woman asked her husband: "Why is it you never make love to me like that?" "Listen," he said, "do you know what Paul Newman gets paid for doing that?"

635.   KIN HUBBARD: "Married life ain't so bad once you get so you can eat things your wife likes."

636.   Judge Roy Bean in marriage ceremonies used to say, "By the authority of the Constitution of the U.S., the State of Texas and the Law west of the Pecos, I, Roy Bean, pronounce you man and wife. May the Lord have mercy on your souls."

637.   "When is your sister thinking of getting married?"
"Constantly."

638.   His wife sounded a little tart yesterday. She asked if he'd ever considered freezing himself until they found a cure for whatever it is he has.

639.   A man and his wife were out driving in the country. He was driving and she was reminiscing. Finally she broke the silence: "John, do you remember when we were first married, and had our first car? Remember how close together we used to sit in that old Ford?" With a twinkle in his eye, the husband replied, "I haven't moved."

640.   "My goodness, everyone knows what a married woman is. That's someone who has nothing to wear and six closets to keep it in."

641.   "I'm going to get a divorce," the man told his friend. "My wife hasn't spoken to me in three months."

I'd think twice about that if I were you," his friend said. "Wives like that are hard to find."

642. Man showing doctor his wife's injured hand: "She did it getting dinner ready last night. It must be frostbite."

643. RODNEY DANGERFIELD: "My wife and I have separate bedrooms, we dine separately, and we take separate vacations. We're doing everything we can to keep our marriage together."

RX for That Ailing Speech

RX #40. Marriage is a great subject to joke about because everyone realizes that underneath the love and understanding that must exist between marriage partners, there also exists a strong competitive drive for individual freedom. Laughter is a form of tension release and few will deny that most marriages on occasion build tension. However, one precaution should be noted about material on marriage. A mixed audience or a predominately female audience will respond quite well to any of the material concerning marriage but a stag male audience, for some strange reason, does not normally respond to this subject with rousing glee. I will leave the reasons for this to the psychologists. Just rest assured that the best place for marriage material is when you have both sets of partners in about equal proportions.

* * * * * *

644. My marriage ain't legal—her Pa didn't have a license to carry a gun!

645. Formerly a man wondered if he could afford to marry; now he wonders if he can get along without a working wife.

646. I'll tell you what our house is like. We have a priest living with us who wanted to get married. The Church sent him over to change his mind.

647.　The couple had just celebrated their golden wedding anniversary. A friend commented to the husband, "I've heard all the women talking about how good you are to your wife." "Well, I haven't always been," confessed the husband. "The first year I made some mistakes. Once I even raised my hand against her and then I couldn't look her in the face for a week." "That so?" "Yes, but after about a week the swelling went down and I could see her just a little bit out of my left eye."

648.　My wife and I started out 25 years ago with absolutely nothing—and we've still got most of that left.

649.　The newlywed groom says he knew his marriage was in trouble very early—when his bride thought "Love, honor, obey" was a multiple choice question.

650.　She is such a bad cook, the garbage disposal thows the food back.

651.　A man who can forget his mistakes is probably married to a woman who doesn't know about them.

652.　Marriage was the first union to defy management.

653.　One housewife to another, "My husband was working in a discount store when I met him. I should've realized then that he was a little off."

654.　She and her husband are inseparable—it takes ten people to pull them apart.

655.　Getting married is like buying on credit. You see something you like, make it your own, and pay for it forever.

656.　If marriages are made in heaven, all their help must be on minimum wage.

657.　An aging sex star tells stage-struck young ladies who want to break into show business to "change your hairstyle, learn how to walk, buy a sexy wardrobe and before you know it, you will be married, have six kids and forget all this nonsense."

658.   When you see who some girls marry, you realize how much they must have dreaded working for a living.

RX for That Ailing Speech

RX #41.   One of the more popular forms of ribbing individuals in the business world today is through the art of insulting, or more properly, roasting. Roasts are fast replacing the company luncheon and club conventions as a form of entertainment. Usually several people participate in the roast, making the job of roaster less demanding on one individual, and making the roast less likely to bomb in the event someone does not have the best of material. However, people are very creative and will generally come up with a few gems that apply to the individual or company being roasted.

A good place to use the comment above (entry 658) would be when introducing the wife of someone being roasted. Have her stand, give the audience time to applaud lightly, then remark, "When you see who some girls marry, you realize how much they must have dreaded working for a living." This gets a laugh without embarrassing the wife and at the same time poking a little good-natured insult in the direction of, what the audience realizes must be a friend. A good comeback on the part of the "roastee" is also expected. The following is a good example.

Because they liked him so much, a large group of friends got together in Louisville one night to verbally assault and drag over the coals Mr. John Elmo "Rabbit" Pace. Roaster after roaster paid reverse-English respects to a man of many parts—a football coach who won 73 percent of all games over a period of 36 years, a teacher whose biology classes were remarkable experiences and a gentleman in every sense of the word. But it was the roastee who, after all the roasters had had their turn, got in the last rapier—the verbal thrust of the evening. "All of you," he said, "have spoken straight from the shoulder—at least, I could determine no higher point of origin!"

*   *   *   *   *   *

659.   My friend Larry claims he married too young. "But," he said, "when you're 59 and in love—what can you do?"

660.   The way to have a happy marriage is for the wife to turn blind and the husband to turn deaf.

661.   Times are tough in Hollywood. People are marrying people they've never married before.

100, 101, 317, 356, 381, 596, 794

MEN

662.   Man has set foot on the top of the moon. Now he needs to lay a hand on his son's bottom.

663.   A man will laugh at a woman trying to put on eye makeup, and yet take ten minutes trying to make three hairs look like six.

664.   The man who has it made is one who has a wife to tell him what to do and a secretary to do it.

665.   When two women meet at a social gathering and press cheek to cheek in what we have come to think of as the Social Kiss, it reminds one of two boxers touching gloves at the bell. When two men meet in similar circumstances, they don't kiss; they look to see where the other keeps his wallet.

666.   A man's salary runs into five figures ... his wife and four kids.

667.   Two ladies overheard: "I wonder what women liked about men—before they invented money." "The same thing men liked about women—before they invented TV."

668. The practical man is the man who knows how to get what he wants. The philosopher is the man who knows what man ought to want. The ideal man is the man who knows how to get what he ought to want.

669. Men may criticize women all they want, but you don't see a woman waste $2 worth of gun shells to get a $1 rabbit; buy a $1 meal and give the waitress a 50¢ tip because of a smile; burn two gallons of gas and spend $25 to hire a boat to go where there aren't any fish.

670. Description of a man of few words: "He never really says anything. Even his bumper sticker is blank."

671. CYD CHARISSE: "The best way to keep a man happy is to treat him like a dog—three meals a day, plenty of affection and a loose leash."

672. Two men from a small town never got along. One became an Admiral, the other a Bishop. Both were out of shape 40 years after high school. They happened to meet at the airport. The Bishop recognized the Admiral and started the old feud again. He said, "Porter, can you tell me when the next plane leaves for Rome?" The Admiral, looking at his fine robes and big stomach, recognized him too and replied, "Madam, it leaves in half an hour, but I think if I were in your condition I wouldn't go."

673. Show me a man who has his two feet planted firmly on God's green earth and I'll show you a man who can't get his pants off.

RX for That Ailing Speech

RX #42. The use of deception is extremely important in delivering a line like the one above (entry 673). To get the maximum effectiveness from this line, try to muster all the sincerity and emotional control at your disposal in building up the individual with sincere and, if possible, well-known facts about the accomplishments of the individual. Then deliver the line above. Both the man and the audience will enjoy the unpected diversion. This also allows the man being honored to be relieved of any embarrassment that he may have modestly felt at being praised. This is a good example of people laughing with you instead of at you, to the delight of all concerned.

* * * * * *

674.   CB radio nuts are strange people. Some men who spend three hours a day talking to total strangers won't say "good morning" to their wives.

675.   The young coed brought a beautiful, curvaceous blonde friend home from college with her for vacation. Introducing her friend to her grandfather the girl added: "And just think, Susie, he's in his nineties." "Early nineties!" the old man corrected.

676.   Men will be boys. Particularly when they're away from their wives.

677.   A wealthy old man struck up a conversation with a pretty girl at a cocktail party. I'm not trying to be fresh," he told her, "but you're one of the cutest young ladies I've ever met and I'd give $50 for just one of your kisses." "How awful," she said. The old man looked alarmed. "Please forgive me," he said. "I didn't mean to offend you." "Oh," she replied, "I'm not offended. I was just thinking of the fortune I've been throwing away."

678.   One day man will be flying on regular rocket trips to vacation on Mars. And his baggage will go on to Venus.

679.   A mature man yearned to fly. Against his wife's objections, he took the necessary lessons and on the day he was to solo pleaded with his wife to come out and watch him achieve this great milestone in his life. Although fearing the worst, she agreed. Full of confidence, the aviator got some last-minute instructions from his grizzled, old instructor, adjusted his goggles, tossed his white scarf over his left shoulder and roared off down the runway. Still anxious and nervous, she stood with the instructor and watched her husband make four missed approaches trying to land. The old veteran turned toward the hanger and over his shoulder quipped to the nervous nellie, "Don't worry ma'am. We can always shoot him down."

680.   If the average man had it to do all over again, he probably couldn't afford it.

681.   A man was sitting in a cab caught in a traffic jam as the meter kept ticking away. After it had climbed a few dollars while the cab stayed in one place, the driver turned around with a sympathetic smile and said, "I know how you feel. I have a son in college."

682.   Howard Hughes did not die. That's just a rumor. Anyone that wealthy would hire somebody to die for him.

683.   Many men stay out of hot water by having a large family and a small water heater.

684.   He held her close as the band played a slow dance. They didn't speak until the music stopped. Then she looked up and whispered: "This dance makes me long for another." He said: "Yeah, me too. But she couldn't make it tonight."

685.   If beer cans were any easier to open, some men wouldn't get any exercise at all.

686.   If the good Lord had created all men equal, we wouldn't need both the long form and the short form.

687.   The big car pulled to a halt in Chicago where a beautiful young thing stood waiting at the bus stop. "Hello," leered the dude at the wheel, "I'm driving west." "Great," said the girl. "Bring me back an orange."

688.   "That means fight where I come from."
"Well, why don't you fight then?"
"Cause I ain't where I come from."

RX for That Ailing Speech

RX #43.   The transition from one subject to another has always been a problem for beginning speakers and is of major concern even to professionals. Suppose you want to go from the subject of automobiles to men. One technique in making the transition smoothly is to simply tell a few stories concerning automobiles and then use the "speaking of" technique. It goes like this, "At least half the drivers of automobiles are men ... speaking of men." After your audience catches on to what you are doing, which usually isn't very long, even the "speaking of" technique becomes instantly recognizable and humorous.

*   *   *   *   *   *

689.   A man who goes from his air-conditioned office in an air-conditioned car to his air-conditioned club in order to take a steam bath is called an Executive.

690.   Some young men today are in favor of the draft. They say it's much better than the bottled stuff.

691.   Three men aged 70, 80 and 90 were asked whom they would like to be buried with. "George Washington," said one. "Abe Lincoln," said another. The third one said, "Elizabeth Taylor." "She ain't dead yet," said one of his friends. "Neither am I," the dreamer shot back.

692.   The man who says he is willing to meet you half way is usually a poor judge of distance.

693.   An auctioneer is a man who signals with a hammer when he has picked your pocket with his tongue.

694.   Two buddies were talking one day and the discussion centered around dreams. The first man started telling of a dream he had the previous night when he went to a ball game and became fast friends with such stars as Mickey Mantle and Hank Aaron. He was a participant in a championship world baseball game, played in an all-star exhibition and later held a press conference immediately following the baseball game. His buddy said he had a different kind of dream. He came home from work and found Elizabeth Taylor and Raquel Welch sitting on his couch with a bottle of champagne. The two suggested that they become close friends so they danced into the wee hours of the night, listening to soft music, sipping champagne, just the three of them. The first man interrupted at this point and asked, "You had two of the most beautiful women there by yourself? Why didn't you call me?" The man replied, "I did but you had gone to a baseball game."

695.   Man blames fate for other accidents, but feels personally responsible when he makes a hole in one.

696.   Never trust a man who scratches one place and itches someplace else.

697.   A diction coach was asked to take on a Miss America contestant from Mississippi. The Southern Belle was a raving beauty but felt she needed to lose her regional accent for national appeal to win the title and a scholarship. Although the coach was warned that she would be an impossible case, the professor confidently replied, "With my perfect diction and a little patience, she will learn by association." After six weeks of intensive training, in a moving graduation ceremony, he announced, "I am so proud of yo progress, mah deah, and heah is yo diploma."

698.   There are lots of men wearing overalls now who

are well bred. The tightness of 'em also shows some are well reared.

699. "So you were engaged to Agnes for five years and then she gave you back your ring? That's what I call a cruel blow." "Oh, it wasn't too bad. In fact, it worked out rather nicely. In the years that Agnes and I were engaged, the ring doubled in value and when she gave it back, I was able to get a better girl with it."

700. Remember the good old days? A man was known for his deeds. Now he is known for his mortgages.

701. No man can serve more than one master. That's the reason you don't see more harems.

RX for That Ailing Speech

RX #44. Will Rogers used to say, "All I know is what I read in the newspapers." The news is still an excellent source of information for us to draw on the subject area of humor. The point is not to look for humor in the news but rather subject categories that lend themselves to a humorous interpretation. For instance, when the Arab oil embargo was at the height of the news media, the above line (entry 701) could have been appreciated perhaps more than at some later date. Keep in touch with world happenings and use this handbook to come up with material that will appear to be ad-libbed for the occasion. It not only makes you look funny but also makes you look smart.

*   *   *   *   *   *

702. He's a man of few words, and even those should be left unsaid.

703. And how about the famous last words of Noah Webster: Zymology, Zymotic and Zymurgy.

704. How about the Englishman looking for a subway in Brooklyn? "I say," he asked a street-wise woman, "when one is in Brooklyn, how does one get underground?" She told him, "Drop dead."

705. I heard of a man who bought himself a $3,000 toupee. Even Jesse James didn't have a price like that on his head.

706. Two men were evidently discussing their families because I heard one of them ask? "Do you have children?" The other answered: "Yes, I have three." "Boys or girls?" The guy answered: "Of course. What do you think, kangaroos?"

707. Two men were trading insults concerning each other's looks. The match was ended with this classic remark: "You're so ugly you'd back a starvin' jackass off a barrel of oats."

708. A fat man and a thin man collided on the street. "From the looks of you there's been a famine around here," said the fat man. "And from the looks of you," replied the thin man, "you caused it!"

709. Two men decided to fight a duel with pistols. One of the men was very, very fat, and when he noticed how thin the other man was, he got pretty excited. He protested, "I'm twice as big a target as he is! I ought to stand twice as far away from him as he stands from me." The thin man agreed, but somehow, they couldn't work it out. So at last the fat man's second said: "Take it easy. I'll fix this." Taking a piece of chalk from his pocket, he drew two lines down the fat man's coat, leaving a space between them. Then he told the thin man, "Now, fire away. But remember, any hits outside the chalk lines don't count."

710. Solomon had 700 wives and 300 concubines. It would seem that any man who would surround himself with all that trouble and strife could not have been gifted with wisdom.

711.   The man who can smile when something's gone wrong has probably just thought of someone he can blame it on.

712.   Show me a man over 50 with his head held high and I'll show you a man with new bifocals.

713.   How tough can things get? A man said he saw a smile button in an antique shop.

13, 14, 33, 259, 332, 457, 587, 626, 717, 1057

RX for That Ailing Speech

RX #45.   Remember that it is the clown that quite often makes people laugh, then makes them cry. Experiment with a wide range of emotions in dealing with humor. Not all humor has to be the slapstick variety in order to be appreciated. The line above (entry 713) can be very thought provoking, the humor therein appreciated but not get a single laugh. Yet people can ponder and appreciate the humor contained in it and smile inwardly. Through your friendly smile and assurance of friendship, you can cause someone to discover a fresh and enlarged concept of the brighter side of life even in a tough situation. Your cheerful attitude can be the roadmap that gives someone else a sense of direction, a more purposeful life and a ray of sunshine in a dismal world. In otherwords, don't be afraid of humor that does not get a laugh if it has thought-provoking qualities that lends itself to the particular situation.

MIDDLE AGE

714.   An old Las Vegas hound reminds you that middle age is that period of life when your idea of getting ahead is staying even.

715.   The change to middle age is when you hear two voices calling you. One says, "Why not?" and the other says, "Why bother."

716. Middle age is when father time catches up with mother nature.

717. A middle-aged lady says unfortunately the men who sit up and notice her nowadays are too old to stand up and follow her.

718. Uncle Fred says that when he was a youngster he was told to listen to his elders. Now that he's an adult, he's told to listen to the youngsters.

719. Everybody hates his own picture in his high school yearbook when it is first published, but 25 years later, glancing through it, he decides he wasn't such a bad-looking kid after all.

720. You're middle aged if, when the air is springy, you're not.

721. Middle age is when your legs buckle and your belt doesn't.

722. DR. O. A. BATTISTA: "A man reaches middle age as soon as he has to throw his shoulders back to maintain his balance."

723. The big shock in becoming middle aged is that you discover you keep on growing older, even after you are old enough.

724. You've reached middle age when pulling your weight is a real drag.

725. GRANDPA JONES, star of Hee Haw: "Middle age is when you feel terrible in the morning and you had no fun at all the night before."

726. Middle age is when you're old enough to know what's good for you but not so old that you do it.

727. Middle age is when you are sitting at home on Saturday night and the telephone rings and you hope it isn't for you.

728.   Middle age is that time in life when we convince ourselves it's only a vitamin shortage.

729.   Middle age is when you feel like the morning after, the night before.

730.   There are two things that never go out of style—a feminine woman and a masculine man, and no matter how the stylists scheme and strive to cover what comes naturally, concealment only seems to emphasize the genuine— like when a woman wears pants but still wiggles where she should and a balding, middle-aged man still thinks he's dangerously attractive to younger women.

171

RX for That Ailing Speech

RX #46.   There is an old saying that "there is nothing new in the world of comedy." The theory is that cavemen probably laughed about the same thing that all of us find humorous today. There is a great deal of truth to that adage. The subject of middle age is something that few of us realizes applies to our own bodies until it sneaks up on us. The fact that others are suffering from the same physical failings makes it a good subject to joke about, provided the majority of the audience has passed through or is approaching middle age. A young audience, however, probably cannot grasp the humor involved in middle age stories since they are thoroughly convinced that they will live forever without maladies. This is perhaps put in perspective by the old saying, "The young think they will live forever, the old fear they will die at any moment." This line in itself is probably appreciated only by the middle aged because they are in a position to see both ends of the spectrum.

MONEY

731. Sure, the 10-cent stamp is gone and the 10-cent cup of coffee is gone, but we still have the 10-cent quarter.

732. There's plenty of money around. The trouble is, everybody owes it to everybody else.

733. There was ten dollars too much in his pay envelope, but Joe said nothing about it. The following week there was ten dollars less in his pay envelope, so Joe went to the accounting office and complained. "Now that you get less money, you bring it to my attention," replied the accountant. "Why didn't you complain last week when you got extra money?" "Well," Joe explained, "anyone can make one mistake. But when it happens two weeks in a row, there's no excuse for it."

734. A boat is a hole in the water surrounded by wood into which one pours money.

735. Being short of cash is a great discomfort. You find it so hard to impress people with your wisdom then.

736. Money isn't everything. It just helps you get into more expensive trouble.

737. PHYLLIS DILLER got off these one-liners in Las Vegas: "Where it used to say 'In God We Trust' on the dollar, it now says 'Lotsa Luck'; food is so expensive that the newest status symbol is Tums; and I told Neil Armstrong that you don't have to be an astronaut to experience weightlessness. Try five dollars worth of groceries in a shopping bag!"

738. There are no idle rich. They're all kept busy dodging people who want some of it.

739. He gets his money the hard way. He has to ask his wife for it.

740. A society matron reports that she was talking to an old-timer to see whether she could hire him to cut her grass. They had some trouble negotiating an amount, so finally she said: "I'll tell you what. Let's just give it a trial—you come to work for me Saturday, and I'll pay you what you're worth." "That doesn't make any sense at all!" he told her indignantly. "I get more than that from Social Security."

741. A collection agency has it's computer to fire off a note that says: "Pay what you owe or we'll tell your other creditors that you did."

742. While money can't buy happiness, it certainly enables you to look for it in comfort.

743. The safest way to double your money is to fold it over once and put it in your pocket.

744. Stopping at the exclusive Washington Plaza Hotel, Mr. Fink asked for some stationery and the clerk asked, "Are you a guest at the hotel?" Mr. Fink indignantly replied, "No, I am NOT a guest. I am paying fifty dollars a day!"

745. If money talks, how come we never heard from Howard Hughes?

RX For That Ailing Speech

RX #47. The key to joking about money is to cover only the very poor or the very rich examples. It is interesting to note that the very frugal are found in both categories and are subject to the same type of humor. Numerous jokes were made about Howard Hughes during his lifetime and for a good while after his death. It is common knowledge that he was one of the wealthiest men in the world and very eccentric. On the other end of the scale, Jack Benny made a career out of appearing to be a frugal sort who had very little money. In both cases, the audience realized the deception but went along with the joke for laughter's sake. The point is this: never use anyone who is moderately wealthy as an example—always reach for the extremes in projecting good, clear humor images.

*   *   *   *   *   *

746. Money ain't everything—but it sure comes in handy when you lose your credit cards.

747. When someone says "it's only money," it's usually *your* money he's talking about.

748. The cashier said that Mr. Rich didn't handle deposits personally, but the woman glared and snapped: "Tell him in this bag I have one million dollars." So Mr. Rich appeared, had the lady to his office, gave her coffee, and called a teller to count the money. "Madam," said the teller, "I must tell you that there is one million, three thousand dollars in this bag, not just a million." "Can I use the phone?" asked the lady. She could. She dialed a number. "Joe," she snarled, "this is Rosie. You dope, you gave me the wrong bag."

749. New Book: *The Short History of Money*. The book has six words ... Here it is. There it goes.

750. It's not that money makes everything good; it's that no money makes everything bad.

751. The person who finds money growing on trees can be sure there has been a great deal of grafting going on.

752. First wife: "Gee, Myrtle, the bank returned my check."
Second wife: "Are you ever lucky. What are you going to buy with it next time?"

753. They say "money talks." Unfortunately, when it hears my name, it says, "Who?"

754. How can we teach our kids the value of money when we can't even teach our Congressmen?

755. The tip you leave for a meal now would have bought it ten years ago.

756. Money still does three things. It does provide some security, promotes leisure and bridges the generation gap.

757. It doesn't make sense. The dollar is floating and we're going down the drain.

RX for That Ailing Speech

RX #48. The best kind of humor is a humanizing form of self-deprecation. That is, an individual poking fun at himself. If you can laugh with people, you can work with them. You can't laugh with people you don't trust. The remark above (entry 757) would be a natural to be used by an economist. This allows the audience to laugh with him, realizing that no one knows all the answers. Rather than admit publically that he or she does not know all the answers and lose the confidence of the audience, the speaker merely eludes to that fact through the use of humor. If your position involves any kind of financial responsibility, try some of the lines about money.

* * * * * *

758. A dollar doesn't go as far as it used to—and it isn't coming as close to us as it used to either.

759. If you want to know what God thinks of money, look at the people he gives it to.

760. Starting from scratch is a lot easier when you have some.

761. Money doesn't talk. It just makes a sonic boom as it goes past.

762.   By the time most of us have money to burn—our pilot light has gone out.

763.   Money used to talk, then it whispered—now it can't even grunt.

764.   The good old days were when you could make $8 a day and spend only $10.

765.   Money isn't everything. It isn't even enough.

766.   The business manager is so tight his wallet is lined with flypaper.

767.   It's easy to tell which folks have the money these days. They're the ones who move before their house is sold.

768.   Hardly anybody these days can make money hand over fist, except a manicurist.

769.   If you want to be remembered, borrow money. If you want to be forgotten, lend it.

770.   The secret of getting rich is learning how to make money faster than you can spend it. From then on it's easy.

771.   Bankers are not stingy. They just have low pockets and short arms.

> **15, 95, 96, 102, 140, 184, 204, 236, 308, 351, 374, 375, 376, 399, 432, 450, 491, 494, 495, 498, 559, 598, 666, 667, 669, 680, 804, 834, 840, 967, 1078, 1091, 1099, 1133, 1193**

MOTHERS

772.   My mother used to grab my ear and lead me on the desired path of action. She called it "child guidance." She called my father's contribution an "uplifting experience."

RX for That Ailing Speech

RX #49. Professional entertainers, speakers, comedians and others who have to address audiences on a regular basis are not the only people who have discovered the value of humor. A monk in a New Jersey monastery regularly does 10 minutes of stand up comedy to relax Catholics during retreat. This is a great idea because it not only allows the audience to forget their problems for awhile but also allows the monk to have some fun while developing his style and technique to be even more effective as a communicator.

The subject of mothers is a good one for anyone to use because of the universal memories of those bitter-sweet childhood days when we were guided along the path to adulthood.

*   *   *   *   *   *

773. Trouble with going through your second childhood is that this time you can't blame your mother.

774. A mother at a drugstore counter recently whirled around to check suspiciously on the activities of her small son. "What are you doing?" she demanded. "Nuthin'," he replied meekly. "Well, quit it," she snapped.

775. Mother's Law: Any time things appear to be going better, you have overlooked something.

776. My parents were always concerned about their kids. My mother waited up for me one night. When I came home, she yelled: "Where were you? I waited so long." I said, "Ma—I was in the Army."

777. My mother used to say: "If only he would wash his neck, I'd wring it."

778. Mothers spend the first part of a child's life getting him to walk and talk, the second part getting him to sit down and shut up.

779. A nurse tells about the young woman who was very embarrassed about giving birth to a baby in the hospital elevator. The nurse said, "Oh, don't feel so bad about that. Why, two years ago, a woman gave birth to a little girl in the hospital parking lot." "I know," sighed the unhappy mother. "That was me, too."

780. His mother left his baby carriage in towaway zones and gave him a feeling of insecurity.

781. My mother used to dose us with sulphur and molasses. I didn't talk until I was 16 years old. I couldn't get my jaws unstuck.

782. All mothers are physically handicapped. They have only two hands.

783. I have found that mothers come in two categories—good housekeepers or good cooks. In my house you could eat off the floor. Most of the time, that's where the food would end up. We would sneak it off our plates and give it to the dog. I wouldn't say Mom was a bad cook, but one year we went through 12 dogs.

NUDISTS

784. You can usually tell the old-timer at a nudist camp. He's the one who brings along a TV set.

785. Ever wonder what a nudist does with the key after he locks his car?

786. ZSA ZSA GABOR: "I hate nudist colonies. I wouldn't go any place where every woman wears the same thing."

787. A guy in a nudist colony was asked what made the greatest impression on him. He replied, "A cane bottom chair."

RX for That Ailing Speech

RX #50.   Here is a clever idea. Some speakers are a little anxious about using humor before an audience of their peers. If a line is not appreciated, the audience may groan and react as if the material personally was the product of the speaker. One way to remain more comfortable with any of this material is to simply admit that you are not sure about the material but you thought you should try to entertain the crowd for at least a few moments so you bought a jokebook at your local bookstore. Then simply hold the book up and read some of the entries to the audience. If you entertain the audience, you will get credit for having made them laugh. If your delivery left something to be desired, they may laugh with you anyway. And, who knows, if your timing is a complete bomb, it may be hilarious. You may find it so comfortable, you will want to adopt the style for your continued use, adding scraps of paper with notes about jokes gleaned from other sources.

*   *   *   *   *   *

788.   The slowest thing in the world is a nudist going through a barbed wire fence.

789.   There'll be more nude bathing at the beaches this summer, and two major ailments are expected to be sunburn and eyestrain.

790.   After a record turnout of volunteer firemen responded to a trash fire at a nudist colony, one firechief commented: "You never saw so many shifty-eyed firemen in your life."

791.   My wife isn't very good at choosing gifts. She once gave a pocket watch to a nudist.

792.   The *New Zealand News*, from down south of the equator, says: "A hole was cut in the wall surrounding a nudist camp. Police are looking into it."

793.   How about the stripper who calls herself, "Nude Math?" She subtracts a little, until she arrives at a very interesting figure.

OPTIMISTS

794.   An optimist is a guy who marries his secretary and expects to continue dictating.

795.   An optimist is one who believes his wife would live on what he made—if he had more.

796.   An optimist is a fellow who knows it is bound to happen, but doesn't think it will happen soon.

797.   Optimists and pessimists both contribute to society. The optimist invents the airplane—and the pessimist adds the parachute.

798.   Definition of a pessimist: An optimist with eight children.

PEOPLE

799.   CARL RIBLET, JR.: "Every person is eager but in a different manner. Some want success, others want fun, and the rest want a lot of both plus a flat stomach and a big appetite."

800.   Things are tough: Ten percent of the people are on welfare, thirty percent on unemployment, and the rest on tranquilizers.

801.   Very few people are fast enough to keep up with their good intentions.

802.   A tactless person is someone who says what everyone else is thinking.

RX for That Ailing Speech

RX #51.   One of the most often asked questions by amateurs is "Should I laugh at my own material?" The answer will vary depending upon the personality of the individual. Some people have a dry sort of wit that enhances the humor of a line simply because they do not react to it. You will have to experiment a little with your personality to find out which method is best suited for your type of delivery. People with a natural, bubbling personality, generally do laugh at their own jokes, quite often even before the punch line, which also enhances the quality of the material.

Keep in mind, however, that a complete reversal of the personality on one or two occasions during a speech may completely break up an audience. For instance, if a stone-faced character has been delivering lines to an audience and the listeners obviously have been reacting favorably, he may bring the house down by breaking up at one of his own punch lines. By the same token, an outgoing personality can create the same effect by delivering a shocking line then freezing his face in a pained or serious expression. In general, do what comes natural to you but don't be afraid to try the opposite on occasions.

* * * * * *

803.   When people are always pinning things on you, maybe you don't have all your buttons.

804.   A bum approached a man and asked for a dime. The man told him he didn't have a dime but he'd be glad to buy his breakfast. "Man," the bum said, "I've had three breakfasts now, trying to get a dime."

805.   People have taken up jogging for one reason or another. One reason is health, the other is to run fast enough to keep their wallets.

806.   A chemist stepped up to the drug counter, hesitated for a moment, and asked for some acetylsalicylic acid. "You mean aspirin," said the druggist sarcastically. "That's right," the chemist replied apologetically, "you know, I never can remember that name."

807.   It's hard to understand what makes people tick. The same kids who refuse to eat spinach grow up and stand in line to buy yogurt.

808.   Hear about the guy who gave up water polo? His horse drowned.

809.   London drivers are more polite. A pedestrian was in a taxi driver's way. He screeched to a halt, leaned out and said, "I say, sir. May I ask what are your plans?"

810.   There are two classes of people. Those willing to work and administrators.

811.   Some people have about as much initiative as an echo.

812.   Fellow got a fortune cookie with both good and bad news. The good news: "You are going to heaven." The bad news: "They are expecting you tomorrow."

813.   People used to settle their problems over coffee and cigarettes—which has now become their problem.

814.   "Do you still smoke six packs of cigarettes a day?"
"Yeh, cough, cough."
"Save the coupons?"
"Yeh, that's how I got the iron lung."

815.   Most people today never had it so good, nor realized that having it so good could create so many new problems.

816.   A guy phones the airport to ask how long it takes to fly to Tulsa.
"Just a minute sir," requested the clerk.
"Thanks," he said and hung up.

817.   During WWII, non-swimmers at naval training stations were required to take swimming lessons after a full day of drill. The chief asked one boy struggling in the water, "What's the matter? Why can't you swim? Haven't you got any water in Georgia?" The floundering recruit replied, "Yes, chief, we've got air, too, but I can't fly."

RX for That Ailing Speech

RX #52.   Some short gems of humor can be used at your discretion if you are cunning enough to take charge at the right moment. The great Soviet clown Oleg Popov is known around the world for his visual antics. However, Popov also has a great verbal sense of humor and has been known to "toast" his backstage admirers with a full shot glass of vodka. One trick he uses is to toss a glass full of vodka high above his head, catch it again without spilling a drop, and in a single swoop empty the contents into his mouth. One of his toasts is, "Let's drink to jokes. Without jokes it is impossible to live in this world. Each man has his own tragedies, but if you tell him a timely joke, that eases his troubles. That's why it is correctly said that one clown is worth a carload of medicine. Let's drink to medicine." Everyone laughs at his excuse to have another drink. Keep a handful of these one- or two-liners in mind and spring them at your convenience as a simple toast to lighten the burdens of others who may have need of this special brand of medicine—the toast.

*   *   *   *   *   *

818.   The trouble with being impartial is people think you don't know what's going on.

819.   "How far were you standing from the deceased when he was shot?"
"86 feet, 6½ inches."
"How can you be so sure?"
"I thought some darn fool might ask me, so I measured it."

820. Everyone can give pleasure in some way. One person may do it by coming into a room, and another by leaving.

821.   "Did you hear about the fellow who invented a device for looking through walls?"
"What does he call it?"
"A window."

822. A report that one of every three American adults is single suggests a vast number of people in this country have cold feet.

823. The stock market is driving people wild. We've been rich and poor before, but not in the same day.

824. "Dad, what is the middle class?" Bobby asked. The father explained: "The middle class consists of people who are not poor enough to accept charity and not rich enough to donate anything."

825. A lot of people who gave up meat for Lent now find they're giving it up for rent.

826. A producer-director of TV commercials in New York was recalling that a young man came in for an audition, announcing that he did bird imitations. "Don't waste my time," snapped the producer, "I don't need any bird imitations in this commercial." "Okay, sorry I bothered you," the young man replied, reaching for his hat. Then he flew out the window.

827. If you haven't made up your mind about reincarnation, just watch the way some people come back to life at quitting time.

828. Seems a man had a terrible night with the pins and told his buddy he was going to throw his bowling ball into the river that night. The next evening, however, the disgruntled bowler was out on the lanes again, rolling them in the gutter. "I thought you said you were going to throw your ball into the river?" asked the friend. "Yeah," replied the bad bowler, "I tried but I missed."

829.   The reason worry kills more people than work is that more people worry than work.

830.   People are divided into two classes: Those who do things, and those who complain that it should have been done some other way.

831.   An Air Chance airplane goes down and lands in the ocean 10 miles from land. The pilot shouts over a microphone, "All those who can swim, get on top of the right wing. All those who can't swim, get on top of the left wing. You people who can swim, start swimming, you are only 10 miles from shore. All those who can't swim, thank you for flying Air Chance."

832.   Some people seem to thrive on looking for something to worry about. I overheard a fellow the other day wondering out loud if the Declaration of Independence had ever been notarized.

RX for That Ailing Speech

RX #53.   The use of satire is extremely important in political situations. A humorist can get by with criticizing his own government or that of other nations as long as his satire is considered humor. Politically, it has been used to enormous advantage by great leaders of the United States. Franklin D. Roosevelt had a colorful sense of humor. Harry Truman also was satirical and used humor to good advantage in pointing out the poor judgment of his opponents. Winston Churchill, extremely gifted in using satire to infuriate both the Germans and the Allies, knew how to make memorable an important point. Victor Borge, the entertainer, used satire against Hitler during his pre-WWII days in Denmark. He became a target of the Nazis and barely escaped arrest in 1940. However, Borge never lost his sense of humor and still uses satire on occasion, believing that "A smile is the shortest distance between two people.

Satire, truth and humor are close allies so try to keep them partners in developing material. For example, if your dark horse candidate in a political race is running much stronger than expected, you can hatefully say, "I told you so" or cheerfully come out smelling like a rose with, "I don't want to say our opposition is worried, but the candidate who was so sure of himself a few days ago now has so many wrinkles in his forehead that he has to screw his hat on."

* * * * * *

833. A compromise has been described as a "deal in which two people get what neither of them wanted."

834. After receiving ten dollars, the fortune teller informed her patron he was entitled to ask two questions. "But isn't that a lot of money for just two questions?" the man asked. "It is," acknowledged the fortune teller. "What's your second question?"

835. Just ask enough people and you'll find some genius who'll advise you to do what you were going to do anyway.

836. The idea some people have of keeping a secret is lowering their voice when they tell it.

837. I can't understand why people are so concerned about cigarette smoking being dangerous to their health when almost nothing you do is much good for it.

838. Asians may not have our sophisticated technology, but if enough people get together, they can become aggressive just because of sheer numbers. For instance, when China first developed an atomic bomb, they had no way to deliver it, so they decided to stand on each other's shoulders and fall across the ocean.

839.   ADLAI STEVENSON: "An editor is a person who separates the wheat from the chaff and prints the chaff."

840.   A tramp was lying under a tree. A motorist asked him for directions to town. He pointed with his foot, "That way." "If you can do a lazier trick than that, I'll give you a dollar," said Mr. Bright. "Put it in my pocket," replied the tramp.

841.   Only in California could you find people having meetings beside the swimming pool discussing how to conserve water during the drought.

> **52, 53, 218, 336, 345, 393, 455, 493, 504, 564, 585, 592, 618, 661, 674, 735, 759, 974, 982, 1056, 1166, 1217**

PHILOSOPHY

842.   Philosophy of a pessimist; he carries a card reading: "In case of accident—I'm not surprised!"

843.   Episcopalians were agonizing over whether to let women become priests. One philosophy was that it would never work because the Catholics would get so jealous they would want male nuns and the world isn't ready for a Sister Fred. According to one broad-minded lady, that was probably true and gave her blessing to use the following quote: "If God had meant for women to be priests, she would have said so."

844.   Penciled on a piece of recycled wrapping paper is a note offering the fatalistic philosophy: "Cast your bread upon the waters today and you wind up with soggy bread and a citation for water pollution."

845.   A barfly philosophized: "I begin thinking about the hereafter, and the prospect of returning to life in another form. And I think I'd like to return ... as a bar of soap in Sophia Loren's shower. I would melt in her presence, of course, but what a tribute to clean living."

846. To err is human; to really foul things up you need a computer.

847. The philosophy of the real estate salesman is much like that of a man or woman seeking a mate. A buyer is sure to turn up eventually even if the listing is expensive, ugly, poorly built and hard to beat.

RX for That Ailing Speech

RX #54. Comparison, through the use of a parable, is an effective way to say things that you might not otherwise have the nerve to utter. It also helps greatly if you smile broadly when using a line like entry 847. Notice also that the remark is non-sexist, since the line cleverly refers to a man or woman seeking a mate. You stand much less chance of offending anyone using this non-sexist term than if you changed the line to read, "A man seeking a wife," or "A woman seeking a husband."

* * * * * *

848. Personally, I didn't realize how expensive beef had become until I saw a two pound steak being delivered in an armored car.

849. In a philosophical discussion a used car salesman commented: "If there is reincarnation, I don't want to come back as a human of any kind." "Why should you?" a friend asked. "You didn't make it the first time."

850. I sure hope New York doesn't go broke. I mean, how would that look? A flag with 49 stars and a hand out?

851. Beware of those catch offers. A free ride may be some place you don't want to go.

852. The sea is looked to as a future source of fuel. For starters, it would help if we could just recover all the oil slicks.

853. Frustration is when your turn comes in the barber shop and you haven't finished the girlie magazine.

854. If you think there are no more new frontiers, just watch a boy ring the front doorbell of his first date.

855. It's so hard to say when one generation ends and the next begins—but it's somewhere between 10 P.M. and midnight.

856. A good listener is one who can give you his full attention without hearing a word you say.

857. An additional joy of giving, rather than receiving, is that you don't have to write thank-you notes.

858. The easiest way to start an argument these days is to get two economists together to try to come up with one theory.

859. A budget is a device for going into debt in an orderly manner.

860. It's easy to have a successful small business today. All you have to do is start out with a successful large business.

861. A budget is like a girdle. Sooner or later everybody wants to get rid of it.

862. My business is like a lover's kiss. When it's good, it's wonderful. When it's bad—it's still pretty good!

RX for That Ailing Speech

RX #55.   The use of a pause is an important consideration in timing for most gags. Take the story above (entry 862), for instance. There is need for only one pause and only in one place. After the line, "When it's bad…" pause to give the mind of the listener a chance to race ahead and dream up all sorts of bad connotations. Then, when the punch line is delivered, the mind has usually completely reversed its line of thinking. The effective use of the pause allowed this humor to develop.

Here's another sample of an effective pause, "I was always joking as a child. When someone was ill in the family, I was sent around to cheer them up. He either died laughing (pause) or died otherwise." Study your material and determine where a pause can be effective. You should also determine where it can kill a story.

* * * * * *

863. Trouble with bucket seats is that not everybody has the same size bucket.

864. They say nothing is impossible, but did you ever try to pin a name tag on a string bikini?

865. Definition of a bore: Someone who deprives you of solitude without providing you with company.

866. An antique is something you can't use that can't be fixed at a price you can't afford.

867. The computer saves a lot of guesswork, but so does the topless bathing suit.

868. What we need is a good barbecue sauce that can also be used as a moustache wax.

869. They say the best is yet to come. With my luck, by the time I get there, it'll be gone.

870. To learn the basic principle of acupuncture, just sit on a tack.

871. Apathy is what you have for everyone. Empathy is what I am supposed to have for you. Sympathy is what others have for us if my empathy doesn't overcome your apathy.

872. Things are always better somewhere else until you get there.

873.　The earth is composed of six layers, like a cake. The similarity is carried even further with all the nuts sprinkled on top.

874.　Prosperity: The period when we enjoy wine, women and song.
　　　Depression: The period when we enjoy beer, mama and TV.

875.　My idea of courage is the guy who has $500,000 invested in the stock market—and turns to the sports pages first.

876.　"Convalescence" is that difficult time when you are better than you were but still not as well as you were before you were as sick as you are now.

877.　A gossip talks about others, a bore talks about himself, but a brilliant conversationalist talks about you.

RX for That Ailing Speech

RX #56.　So much of humor depends on the subject. Some subjects have low interest and must be built up through clever conversation, other subjects are of high interest and require very little more than brief mention. However, everybody's favorite subject is themselves. That's why this comment (entry 877) is not only satirical humor, it is truth. A person's name is generally his most precious commodity. About all you have to do is mention it and you get their attention. Imagine the outrageous laughter created when W. C. Fields delivered this line in his unique style at a function honoring Will Rogers: "I never met a man I didn't like except Will Rogers." This is a strange mixture of admitting public jealousy on the one hand and praising the talents of the individual on the other. At any rate, it certainly got Will Rogers' attention.

*　*　*　*　*　*

878.   A deficit is what you have when you haven't as much as you had when you had nothing.

879.   Acupuncture: On the jab training.

880.   What do we need cotton for? Oh yeh, to stuff in the ends of aspirin bottles.

881.   Cooperation is doing what you would rather not with a smile.

882.   He who hesitates is not only lost, he also gets rear-ended.

883.   Have you ever noticed that what is called "congestion" on a bus is called "intimacy" in a night club?

884.   Confucious in 529 B.C.: "He who will not economize will have to agonize."

885.   The greatest obstacle to overcome in carrying out your own plans is good advice.

886.   Confidence is a feeling you have before you really understand the problem.

887.   When I face that great computer in the sky, let it be written that though I was spindled and mutilated—I did not fold.

888.   Memory is what makes you wonder what you forgot to do.

889.   Meat prices are so high people are trying to find a Hamburger Helper Helper.

890.   Making a comfortable living these days is like licking bourbon off cactus.

891.   Nowadays when you hear of someone making his living from the soil, it's probably the owner of a laundromat.

892.   Two can live as cheaply as one ... if one doesn't eat.

RX for That Ailing Speech

RX #57.   It has been said of many humorists that they are not specifically funny men or women, but tellers of funny material. Many amateurs and professionals alike are merely commentators who use humor to illustrate their comments. If the economy is bad, inflation is rampant, food is expensive and all of this is on everyone's mind, the humor in a remark that turns the tables on the old adage can be readily appreciated. With a little imagination you can probably come up with original material of your own, by just tacking on an extra comment to an old saying or proverb. For instance, "The lion and the lamb shall lie down together ... but the lamb won't get much sleep."

*   *   *   *   *   *

893.   Two can live as cheaply as one but only for half as long.

894.   There's the egghead community where you need an IQ of 110 to qualify as village idiot.

895.   A greeting card company is out with an economy line—for people who don't deserve the very best.

896.   I believe in living within my income—even if I have to borrow to do it.

897.   "You're pretty close to an idiot!"
"All right then, I'll just move over a little bit!"

898.   The closest one can come to understanding eternity is to try to catch up with the Jones'. Once you catch them, you find they have refinanced.

899.   Memory is what reminds you of something you forgot without telling you what it is.

900.   When the meek inherit the earth, it will be my luck to get part of New York City.

901.   KIN HUBBARD: "It's going to be fun to watch and see how long the meek can keep the earth after they inherit it."

902.   It would be okay if the meek inherited the earth if we could be sure they would remain meek after they got it.

903.   Three things in this world are unexpected—triplets.

904.   Show me a harpist, and I will show you a plucky musician.

905.   Look at it this way, when you think of all the things in life that you wanted but didn't get—think of all the things you didn't want and didn't get.

906.   You become well-to-do by doing what you do well.

907.   The most embarrassing thing that ever happened to me came about because the publishers of "Who's Who" asked me to submit a resumé of my life and accomplishments. In filling it out I discovered that I didn't even qualify for What's What.

RX for That Ailing Speech

RX #58.   A point that should never be forgotten is that one should never unwittingly try to use humor to hurt someone or create an emotionally tense situation. If you are going to kid a group, be sure to kid all of them equally. And even more importantly be sure to include yourself. This puts everybody on equal footing and will make many points for you. Your ideas may also stimulate some action in the right direction even though people may accept your remarks as a guest. A famous example is that of Will Rogers who talked about President Calvin Coolidge for years without alienating the President. Many humorists of the day were criticizing Calvin Coolidge for being a do-nothing President. Will Rogers pointed out that he never criticized the President for that because Coolidge could do it better than anyone else. The beloved humorist always got away with these kinds of remarks because he made light of himself in the same humorous way.

* * * * * *

908. Wisdom could be defined as having the means to make a fool of yourself and not doing it.

909. A wish for special occasions: In the truck garden of life, may your pea pods never be empty.

910. Nothing is certain in this world except death, taxes and teenagers.

911. If more than one mouse is mice—it seems that more than one spouse would be spice ...

912. HERBERT HOOVER: "Blessed are the young for they shall inherit the national debt."

913. Considering all the medicare, welfare and social security, if you aren't sick, poor or old, you just don't have a future.

914. Patrick Henry shouted, "Give me liberty or give me death." The next generation shouted, "Give me liberty." Then came the generation shouting, "Give me."

915. EARL WILSON: "Hollywood is where they take a girl from Ohio, give her a Spanish name and send her to England to make a movie about the French Revolution."

916. Answer "true or false." Monday is a heck of a way to spend one seventh of your life.

917. Worry is like a rocking chair. It gives you something to do, but won't get you anywhere.

918. Now there is a "Skier's Anonymous" Club. If you have a craving to ski, you call them and they send a guy over to break your leg.

919.   If God had meant for Texans to ski, he would have given them a mountain.

920.   Let a smile be your umbrella and you'll get a mouthful of rain.

921.   The real reason solar energy has never made it as a substitute for gas and electricity is that the utility companies still haven't figured out a way to put a meter on the sun.

922.   Playing the stock market is like taking pins out of a new shirt. No matter how careful you are, there's a chance you'll get stuck.

RX for That Ailing Speech

RX #59.   One thing that any speaker, particularly a humorist, must establish very early in his presentation is the ability to be in command of the audience. People will laugh at your material if they respect you as a likable, carefree, thoughtful, witty individual. However, make no mistake about it, an audience loves to run "roughshod" on an amateur and will show no pity on one that does not have complete command of the situation. For this reason, it is important to start out with something simple that subconsciously commands the allegiance of the audience to you as a leader. One old trick in establishing command of the situation is to have the audience applaud at the right spot for a well-done story or piece of material.

Here's one way to do that. Start out with a line something like, "Some of the things I'm going to say here today are going to be hilariously funny or of tremendous socio-economic importance to each and every one of you. Please feel free to applaud when either of these situations come about. Just in case I'm wrong about that could I please accept my applause now rather than risk waiting until the end." Then smile and politely lead or wait for the applause and look with great expectation toward the audience. Without a doubt they will applaud. If you do this in a clowning manner, you've not only developed rapport with the audience but subconsciously established yourself in a position of control.

* * * * * *

923. Seems like all public servants are threatening to strike. They ought to star in a municipal production called "What's My Whine?"

924. There is one thing about stupidity: You can be fairly sure that it is genuine.

925. Oratory is the art of talking at length without letting on what you are talking about.

926. If the safety pin had been invented today instead of long ago, it would have six moving parts, two transistors and require a serviceman.

927. Nothing is quite so annoying as to have someone go right on talking when you are interrupting.

928. Nothing makes it easier to resist temptation than a proper bringing up, a sound set of values—and witnesses.

929. There is an old proverb that comes to mind whenever I am presented with a gift: "Thanks for the next one. This one I've got."

930. Wouldn't it be great if all the countries of the world were as friendly as the travel folders say they are?

931. A tip for those going abroad. In an undeveloped country, don't drink the water. In a developed country, don't breathe the air.

932. Thought for today: Starting from scratch isn't as hard as starting without it.

933. If water pollution gets any worse, walking on it will be a cinch.

934. Praise is something someone tells you about yourself that you suspected all along.

935. Anything worth doing is worth putting off to make sure.

936. Some price tags represent value—others nerve.

937. There has been little real progress in the last 6,000 years. It even took Noah 40 days and nights to find a parking place.

RX for That Ailing Speech

RX #60. Man's success in life is largely determined by his ability to dream, to visualize and then to master a dream so it becomes an actuality. Today and ever since the world began, men of vision have needed to be heard. Many of them miss out on the wonderful things in their everyday experience, lucrative opportunities, glorious occasions because they cannot communicate their ideas in a way which is anxiously listened to by their peers. Connect your humor to your ideas as a carrier and realize that success can come to those who dream, visualize, and communicate. Use these humorous stories not only to entertain but to make a point, and you are well on the way to successful communication.

* * * * * *

938. It's no longer a sin to be rich—it's a miracle.

939. Better to have loved a short girl than never to have loved a tall.

940. You're never quite sure what kind of a mind anybody has until he gives you a piece of it.

941. Luxury: Something you do without until getting it, but by that time it has become a necessity.

942.   No matter how love sick you may be, don't take the first pill that comes along.

943.   I just can't get used to seeing a beard and pony tail on the same head.

944.   It's not what you know that counts, but what you think of in time.

424, 594

POLICE

945.   If aerosol cans are banned, will the police be reduced to using roll-on Mace?

946.   A rookie policeman was asked, in an oral exam, what he would do to disperse a threatening mob. After a few mintues of thoughtful concentration, he looked up brightly and said, "I'd start to take up a collection."

947.   They gave me a police escort from the airport to this meeting. Whew!! It's not easy to run between two motorcycles!

948.   A state policeman stopped a speeding woman driver. He snapped: "Don't you know you can't drive over 55?" She snapped back: "I'm only 53!"

949.   RODNEY DANGERFIELD admitted that he lives in a pretty rough neighborhood: "The other day, a guy was fleeing from the scene of the crime and a cop was running about ten paces ahead of him."

950.   A police dispatcher answered the phone. The conversation went like this: "Hello. I'd like to report my missing husband." "Can you describe him, please?" "Well, he's very short, bald, he's fat, he has a high-pitched voice, a five-day growth of whiskers, and ... ah, the heck with it!"

951.   Did you hear about the student who graduated from the police training program at the top of his class? They called him a Phi Beta Copper.

952.   The sergeant took the rookie patrolman to his beat, telling him, "You see that red light way up the street? You cruise between here and that light." The young patrolman did not show up at headquarters for a week. When he did come in, he was rumpled, completely beat. "Where in the world have you been?" his superior asked. "Sergeant," the rookie said shakily, "you know that red light you showed me? Well, that was on a truck headed for Philadelphia."

342, 552, 792, 1250

RX for That Ailing Speech

RX #61.   Always use your material with a positive outlook as far as the expected response from an audience is concerned. Always be an optimist, enthusiastic, confident, never pessimistic nor discouraging. Deliver your lines with a cheerful attitude and hope for the best. Hope, the best of all medicines, is powerful medicine. Just as a dog can sense a human's sincere affection for him, an audience can sense your optimistic attitude in their reception of your material.

POLITICIANS

953.   Our favorite politician stands about as much chance of getting re-elected as Dolly Parton does of drowning.

954.   An old pro in the state department has concluded the international situation is as hard to handle as an armful of coat hangers.

955.   Some of our politicians change sides as often as a windshield wiper.

956.   They're saying that the House of Representatives used to get work done when drinking was still fashionable.

957.   Will Rogers' adivce: "If you can't convince 'em, confuse 'em."

958.   A mother and father were worried about what profession their son would choose. A friend told them to place on the dining room table a $20 bill, a Bible and a fifth of liquor. Then, they were to hide behind the draperies and observe their son's actions when he came in. If he took the $20 bill, he would grow up to be a banker. If he chose a Bible, a preacher; and if he chose the fifth of booze, a drunkard. Well, the son came in and put the $20 bill in his wallet, tucked the Bible under one arm and the fifth under the other, and strolled out of the room. "Great goodness, Martha," said the husband, "he's going to be a politician!"

959.   Every American boy can go into politics and he can grow up to be Vice President. It's just one of those chances he has to take.

960.   A prominent Russian newspaper announces that it is running a contest for the best political joke. First prize is 20 years.

961.   President Grover Cleveland, the only President to take a bride while he was in office, found that the creakings and sounds (of the Old White House) in the still of the night frightened his young wife. One night, the terrified President's wife awakened him and whispered, "Grover, there's a burglar in the house." "Don't let that alarm you, my dear," answered the President. "There's a dozen in the Senate!"

962.   An honest politician is one who when he's bought stays bought.

963.   He's a perfect politician—he's spent half of his life making promises and the other half making excuses.

964.   A country woman told a politician after an appearance, "Your speech was superfluous." Congressman Moorehead's eyebrows went up a bit but he recovered quickly, and answered with a grin, "Why, thank you. I'm thinking of having it published posthumously..." The woman was ecstatic. "Oh, that's wonderful! And the sooner the better!"

965.   Being Vice President is like adding maternity benefits to Social Security—you're there but nobody needs you.

966.   A visitor to Washington parked his car near the Capitol. As he stepped out he said to a man standing nearby, "If you are going to be here for a few minutes, will you keep an eye on my car?"
"Do you realize that I'm a U.S. Senator?" asked the bystander.
"No, I didn't know," said the motorist, "but it's all right. I'll trust you anyway."

967.   One senator to another: "You spend a billion here, a billion there, and the first thing you know, it adds up."

RX for That Ailing Speech

RX #62.   It is extremely important to put on a happy face when delivering material of a happy nature. Even if your heart is breaking, it is important to let the outside world see only the positive side of your thoughts. It's not only good public relations, it's good medicine for your health and the health of others. Smiling can help you be better at your job, a more effective parent and in general, enjoy life more. Some studies, for instance, have indicated that the frowning physician faces twice as many malpractice suits as the open, smiling doctor.

Another study revealed that 80 percent of the parents of juvenile delinquents were habitual non-smilers. In delivering your material, try to consciously start out, or incorporate at decent intervals, the simple smile. It is just one of a broad range of ways we give each other feedback. A smile that is sincere and from within tells the world we're okay and so are the other inhabitants of it. This can be extremely important in large urban areas where things are more impersonal. However, if smiling does not come naturally for you, don't force it. Especially don't be a sour puss in private and a ray of sunshine on the platform. If you use the smile, and most people should, develop a true sense of appreciation for it by using it in both public and private.

*   *   *   *   *   *

968.   There are two sides to every question but some of the questions windily debated by politicians are like base drums: After you listen to both sides, you still haven't heard much.

969.   A reporter asked Senator Fogbottom for a comment on the hearing.

Senator: "Is this off the record or on record?"
Reporter: "Off the record."
Senator: "Off the record, I can't comment on that."

970.   Democrats buy most of the books that have been banned somewhere.

Republicans form censorship committees and read them as a group.

971.   Definition of a politician: He never met a tax he didn't hike.

972.   A political candidate took a cheap shot at an opponent, saying, "He's the son of a rich man. Here he is, 43 years old, and he's never worked a day in his life." After the debate, an old fellow walked up to the rich man and asked, "You the feller who's never worked a day in his life?" The wealthy aspirant for office admitted he was indeed. "Wal, let me tell you something, sonny," said the old man. "You ain't missed nothin.'"

973.   Politician: A man who thinks twice before saying positively nothing.

974.   You can't fool all of the people all of the time—but some politicians figure that once every four years is good enough.

975.   The conversation was about a prominent politician. "His honesty," someone said, "has never been questioned." Pause. "As a matter of fact, it's never been mentioned."

976.   A speaker at a political rally said to the congregation: "Before we send this man's soul to Washington, can we have a good word about him?" There was complete silence. He asked again, imploringly: "Can we have a good word about this man before we send him up North?" No one answered. Again he pleaded, and finally a little old man got up and said, "His brother was worse!"

977.   I went to a football game, and at half time, the marching band paid tribute to the current Administration—by forming a giant unemployment line!

978.   Then there's the politician who felt he got up one morning on the wrong side of the country.

979.   A group of barnstorming supporters of two political opponents for President wound up in the same small town on a Sunday. They all went to the only church in town. After the service, a kid asked his father why the preacher said a special prayer for the politicians. He replied, "He didn't son. He looked them over and then prayed for the country."

980.   A candidate was complaining that his opponent

was telling lies about him. His campaign manager told the guy to let well enough alone. "He might start telling the truth about you."

981. The trouble with politics is that the winners get the jobs, the losers get the ax, and nobody takes down the campaign posters.

982. Trouble with politics is that all the people who can do it better, never come out and do it.

RX for That Ailing Speech

RX #63. People who do not have a natural sense of humor or those with an extremely analytical mind are often overly inquisitive about the structure of a joke and just what it is. For those to whom humor comes easily an explanation is usually not needed nor sought. However, for those more deeply involved in the analysis of humor, an explanation of a joke may be helpful in developing and nourishing the ability to relate verbally the surprise element so necessary in the punch line. The basic idea of a joke becomes somewhat clearer with an effort to visualize it in a completely analytical way.

The theory requires, in one example, an arrangement of geometric surfaces at different levels and a point moving along one surface until it suddenly plunges or rises to another surface. As strange as it may seem, this rise or plunge marks the convergence of conditions that give rise to catastrophes. The catastrophe can be a riot in unexpected surroundings, an explosion in a place where explosions would be completely unexpected, deodorant failure in the midst of an important occasion. In this application of theory to humor, the surfaces represent different levels of meaning, the edge of the surface is the point and the rise or plunge represents the punch line. For those to whom analysis is important, this explanation may be helpful. For those to whom humor needs no explanation, it may be disregarded.

417

PRESIDENT

983.   The man who said he would rather be right than President probably realized the impossibility of being both.

984.   "Do you think the President is a man of the people like they say?"
"I guess so. He seems as confused as the rest of us."

985.   And speaking of specials, the President brought a new spirit into the White House—and his brother drank it.

986.   The President recently commented on the molder of national opinion. "Why, our economy is in much better shape than people think," said the chief executive. "If I weren't President, I would be investing heavily in the stock market." "Yes," replied the Vice President, "if you weren't President, so would I."

987.   The President is donating his important papers to his old Alma Mater. They will be displayed under glass in a Dixie cup.

988.   FDR had his famous cigarette holder. With LBJ, it was the ten-gallon hat. With Jerry Ford, it was the Band-Aid. With Carter, it's a smiling personality the people respect—his brother Billy.

989.   There is a new toy car on the drawing boards for election years. It is to be called the "Presidential Model." It looks good but you don't know when it's going to run. The "Deluxe Model" runs even when you don't want it to.

990.   One U.S. President had his speeches written at the intellectual level of a nine-year-old. President Truman used to read his speeches in bed to his wife. Anything Bess didn't understand, he changed.

273, 356, 499, 960

PSYCHIATRISTS

991.   A man went to see a psychiatrist with a chicken on his head.

The chicken asked, "Can you get this guy out from under me?"

992.   Seems an elderly man was being examined for possible admission to a mental health facility. A psychiatrist was talking to him in an effort to determine the clarity of the man's thinking. "My office is out that door and down the hall to the right," the doctor said. "Go down there and see if I'm in my office." Without showing any surprise, the patient fired off a quick answer. "There's the phone," he said, pointing to the doctor's desk. "See for yourself!"

993.   Psychiatrists who tell parents to spend more time with their children may be simply trying to drum up more business.

994.   Hear about the psychiatrist who went to Las Vegas to make only mental bets and lost his mind?

995.   Psychiatrists say it's not good for a man to keep too much to himself. The IRS says the same thing.

996.   He went to a psychiatrist because he thought he was ugly. The psychiatrist made him lie on the sofa— face down.

997.   He's improving—his psychiatrist lets him sit up on the couch.

135

RX for That Ailing Speech

RX #64.   Throughout this handbook you will find little bits and pieces of encouragement and motivation. It is extremely important for the student of humor to maintain a very serious motivation for developing his ability to be funny. If you want to become a lawyer, there are schools requiring a certain number of years to devote to the proper training. The same thing applies for numerous other professions such as medicine, teaching, preaching, etc.

However, for most of us there is no place that you can go to learn comedy. It must become a personal commitment on your part and it will not come easy. Flip Wilson, for instance, started reading to get the opinions of great comedians and comics to determine how many years it takes for a great comedian to get his act together. The general opinion, according to Wilson, is 15 years. In the first 11 years as a comedian, things were not so funny on the financial side for Flip Wilson. He reportedly earned $700 annually during that period of time. So take a lesson from a pro, keep motivated, keep studying, serve your apprenticeship.

RELIGION

998.   My family was the only Irish family in my neighborhood. I was a choir boy until I was 33 years old. We had a very small parish, our bingo board only had 11 members. We did all right, though. Father O'Malley, our pastor, used to holler the numbers out in Latin so the Protestants wouldn't win.

999.   We lived so far back in the country our Catholic church couldn't afford a priest. All they could get was a step-father.

1000.   A notice in a church paper announced: "Tuesday afternoon there will be meetings in the north and south ends of the church. Children will be baptized at both ends."

1001.   Shaking hands with the minister after the service, a woman exclaimed: "Wonderful sermon! Everything you said applies to somebody or other I know."

1002. A priest with both arms in a cast runs into two long-haired hippies who inquire about the accident. "Fell in the bathtub," explained the priest and went on his way. Later one of the hippies asked the other, "Hey, what is a bathtub, anyhow?" "How should I know? I'm not a Catholic."

1003. Minister: "I hear you went to the ballgame instead of church last Sunday."
Man: "That's a lie—and I've got the fish to prove it!"

1004. A preacher's son was taught to always say a prayer to help him through any difficulty. He was prying the lid off a barrel of molasses to get a finger dipping lick or two when he slipped and fell in. He prayed, "Oh, Lord, grant me a tongue to match this opportunity."

1005. A nervous young preacher stood before a congregation to preach his first sermon. Sweating and stammering, he said, "F-f-f-friends, when I came here tonight only the Lord and myself knew what I was going to preach. And now only the Lord knows."

1006. New pastor: "What did you think of Sunday's sermon, Mrs. Jones?"
Member: "It was great, preacher. We didn't know what sin was until you came here."

1007. A four-year-old offered to give the golden text at Sunday School when the teacher asked for a volunteer from the class. He recited, "Don't be scared. It ain't nobody but me!" The actual verse—from Mark 6:50—reads: "It is I. Have no fear."

1008. An ancient holy man continually preached that the rich should share their wealth with the poor. His wife asked him what success he was having and he told her: "I'm halfway to my goal—the poor have consented to accept."

1009. A minister recently announced that there are 726 different kinds of sin. He is now being besieged with requests for the list, mostly from folks who think they're missing something!

1010. Did you hear about the liberal church out in California? It has four commandments and six suggestions.

1011. We ought to feel sorry for atheists. When they die, they'll be laid out, all dressed up ... and no place to go.

1012. There's the innovative priest who has a Fast Confessional Line for those with three sins or less.

1013. Being a Baptist won't keep you from sinning but it will keep you from bragging about it.

29, 212, 214, 216, 219, 556, 1062, 1072, 1074

RX for That Ailing Speech

RX #65. How many times have you said to someone, "Something just told me to say that." This is instinct or intuition. It is also called the nose of the mind, the untaught ability, intelligence incapable of self-consciousness. It is that certain something which tells a person when the time has come to act. It gives impulses, hunches or strong feelings to do one thing or another. So much of humor is that way. In reading through this material, don't try to analyze the source of the humor. When something tells you that a story or line is good, put a mark beside it and use it. Your intuition seldom will let you down.

RELATIVES

1014.   The family took Grandpa to see a show starring the Rockettes, the beautiful, scantily clad showgirls of Radio City Music Hall fame. When asked what he thought of the show, he said, "Seven of them girls has had appendicitis."

1015.   My uncle received a call from a bill collector. He told him that he took all the bills due, shook them in a hat, and let a little girl draw one. "Hell, man, your name ain't come up yet," he said.

1016.   My grandfather, who is deaf, decided that a hearing aid was too expensive, so he got an ordinary piece of wire and wrapped it around his ear. "Do you hear better now with that wire around your ear?" a friend asked. "No, but everybody talks louder."

1017.   My uncle was asked the difference between a recession and a depression. "Well," said my uncle, "if you take a vise, put your finger in it, turn it till you can't stand it any more, that's recession. If you turn it once more, that's depression."

1018.   The boss commented to an employee, "Heard you had a big fire at your house?" The worker said, "We sure did. My mother-in-law lit all the candles on her birthday cake."

1019.   A road map is often what my aunt uses to find out how she got to where she wasn't going.

1020.   My aunt and uncle are advertising for their lumber yard. He brags about his wooden leg and her cedar chest.

1021.   We had a power failure over at our house last night. My mother-in-law lost her voice.

1022. My grandfather says that ignorance is like a gold tooth. It is impossible to display it if the mouth is shut.

1023. When and if you get rich you will, of course, possess many things in large numbers, such as cash, stocks, bonds, jewels, real estate—and relatives.

1024. My uncle says that leisure time is when his wife can't find him.

1025. Relative to the difference between a rebate and a kickback: "A rebate is something I am entitled to, and a kickback is something that is given to somebody else."

1026. My cousin could have had any girl he pleased. Trouble is he has never pleased one.

1027. My uncle went in for a cup of coffee and the service was so slow it was 30 minutes before he noticed they had topless waitresses. That's as bad as the guy whose job became obsolete—he was selling sneakers to streakers.

1028. My brother-in-law was complaining the other night that the state of the economy has caused him some hardship, depriving him of a certain distinction he enjoyed by being unemployed.

9, 101, 106, 127, 156, 190, 263, 282, 352, 427, 568, 573, 629, 637, 646, 675, 718, 1205

RX for That Ailing Speech

RX #66. A great deal of patience and wisdom is needed in developing humor. Patience is a necessary ingredient of all great achievements. The great inventors and scientists are people who never gave up, who tried again and again until success came their way. Patience has taught mankind to bear everyday trials and tribulations. It builds character to solve big problems when and if they come.

Have patience in developing your material in the same way. Do not try a line or a story once and give up on it. Try it several times until it has been given a fair chance for evaluation. You will soon find that most material will receive the proper response once you have developed the patience to try it, evaluate it, use it in the most effective way. As the old saying goes, "A hand full of patience is worth more than a bucket full of brains."

RESTAURANTS

1029. "You have a very clean restaurant," remarked the patron to the owner.

"Thank you," replied the owner, "and what in particular prompted you to say this"

"Everything tastes like soap."

1030. A bartender was helping wait on tables during the evening rush in a plush grill and he wasn't liking it much. A gourmet asked him, "Do you have frog legs?" "No," replied the bartender, "I walk this way because my pants are too tight."

1031. Sign seen at a restaurant: "We don't serve women. Bring your own."

1032. "Is that restaurant as popular as ever?"

"No, nobody goes there anymore. It's too crowded."

1033. How about that Japanese quick-lunch restaurant where you only have to take off one shoe?

1034. A new dinner theater opened in town—the play was a comedy and the dinner a tragedy.

1035. Some restaurants have such rude waiters their slogan ought to be "Eating out is fun. Eat someone out today."

1036. A restaurant owner says, "The best way to serve spinach and prunes is to somebody else."

1037. Melvin says he ate in a restaurant the other night that was so bad the Humane Society doesn't let it give out doggie bags.

1038. In a restaurant a fellow ordered Idaho potatoes, and complained that they were very small. Then he took a bite and said they tasted terrible. The waiter replied, "Lucky they're small, ain't it?"

1039. Dialogue at a greasy spoon: "Waitress, there's a dead fly in my soup!" "Yes, sir, it's the heat that kills them."

1040. There is a new restaurant called "Jaws." Costs you an arm and a leg to eat there.

1043, 1061, 1194, 1195, 1198

SALESPEOPLE

1041. The best "top salesman" we ever heard of was the one who sold two milking machines to a farmer with only one cow and then took the cow as a down payment.

1042. Did you hear about the world's worst salesman? He couldn't sell a cold beer to Billy Carter.

1043. A salesman, seating himself in a restaurant one morning, told the waitress, "I want two eggs fried very hard, two pieces of toast burnt black, and a cup of weak, lukewarm coffee." "Okay, if you're sure that's what you want. Anything else?" "Yes, I want you to sit down and nag me," he said, "I'm homesick."

RX for That Ailing Speech

RX #67.   One well-known comedy writer for many of the famous radio and television shows, Phil Leslie, explained his theory of humor: "To write comedy, you have to be able to write fairly good drama and then add the laughter." Leslie explains that his comedy sources are varied. Sometimes just one word from an unsuspecting friend sparks an idea. This is great advice to keep in mind.

Professional writers write material for actors who are not necessarily gifted in developing humor. However, many good actors become comedy personalities because they are able to play out the drama and then recite the punch line in the correct place that brings out the humor in a situation. Keep this in mind when delivering your own tidbits of laughter to an unsuspecting individual or audience. If a word sets your fantasy in motion, play out the drama, pretend you are serious and deliver the punch line with the proper timing. If they laugh, you are a hero. If they don't, just pretend it was pure drama and nobody will be the wiser. The audience will let you know whether or not your material and timing have created drama or comedy.

*   *   *   *   *   *

1044.   "Are you sure these field glasses are high-powered?" a customer inquired. The ambitious salesman responded: "Lady, when you use these glasses, anything less than ten miles away looks as if it were behind you."

1045.   A saleslady in a hat shop gushed: "That's a darling hat. Really, it makes you look ten years younger." The customer retorted: "Then I don't want it. I can't afford to put on ten years every time I take off my hat!"

329, 442, 847, 849

SCIENTISTS

1046.   With all the artificial sweeteners around, medical science is now bracing itself for another human ailment. Artificial diabetes.

1047.   Scientists fed 40 pounds of sweetener per day to a rat and it died. That sucker exploded all over the lab.

1048.   A distinguished scientist was participating in a panel discussion with other learned scholars on the results of a comprehensive study of the nation's future water supply which he and his colleagues had just completed. "Gentlemen, I have some good news and some bad news for you. Our study shows that by the year 2000 everyone in the U.S. will be drinking recycled sewage from his home water tap." "Great Scott!" came a shout from the audience. "Quick, tell us the good news." "That was the good news," replied the scientist. "The bad news is that there won't be enough to go around."

1049.   Scientists have discovered great things, but they haven't yet brought to light why a woman's slip sags down and a man's shirt creeps up.

1050.   Scientists in Wyoming report coyotes won't bother sheep if the sheep taste funny. You'd think that just being tasted might upset them a little.

1051.   Scientists are making tremendous strides. They have sent men to the moon. They have sent men orbiting around the earth. They have sent men from two different countries to rendezvous about earth. And they have stopped polio in its tracks. Maybe some day they will be able to tell us why an 11-year-old boy can't walk around a mud puddle.

1052.   It seems that the NASA space center in Houston

was sending around samples of moon rocks for all the smart scientists at land-grant universities to study. By the time they got around to the Midwest schools, all the moon rocks were gone. So they went out onto a Texas feedlot, took soil samples and sent them to two leading universities. Their scientists just about went crazy analyzing those samples. Finally, they got together, conferred for an extended time, and announced that, "The cow indeed did jump over the moon."

294

SECRETARIES

1053.   While two janitors were cleaning up a business office late one night, one exclaimed, "Just look at this!" He uncrumpled a sheet of paper from a wastebasket and said, "Misspellings, erasures, smudges, skip-spacing ... Boy, this secretary must really be built!"

1054.   "Miss Wilcox, always add a list of figures at least three times before you show me the results." "Mr. Johnson, I have added these figures ten times." "Good. I like my secretary to be thorough." "And here are my ten answers."

1055.   The boss told his new, slow-thinking secretary he'd be in conference and didn't want any telephone calls. "If they say their business is important," said the boss, "just say, 'that's what they all say.'" That afternoon his wife called and said, "I must talk to him. I'm his wife." "Yeah," said the secretary, "That's what they all say."

1056.   Twice as many people are engaged in clerical work now as there were in the 1940s. Maybe we don't know what's going on, but we're getting it all down on paper.

1057.   Men who complain of laboring under a heavy burden at the office ... should hire a lighter secretary.

1058.   She doesn't take dictation very well but it really doesn't matter. Anything you'd want to say to her, you wouldn't want in writing anyway.

157, 246, 664, 794

RX for That Ailing Speech

RX #68.   One of the interesting things about humor is that it knows no age barriers for the teller. In most occupations, a man or woman is forced to retire at a certain age because he or she loses efficiency as an employee. In the case of humor, this seems to work in the opposite direction. If you are a very young person, you may even find some difficulty in selling your humor because your personality may make it come across as cockiness or a brash know-it-all. As you get older, you find that people tend to react to your remarks, especially humorous ones, as if you were a sage. So take heart, the older you get the more you will be appreciated for your ability to laugh at life and all of the human failings that accompany advanced age. A professional quarterback is considered old at age 35 but think of the great comedians who went out on top, or were still going strong well past eight or nine decades. Groucho Marx, Jack Benny and George Burns are just a few. So no matter what your age, start now to build your material and style and keep it going. There is no end in sight.

SIGNS

1059.   A sign in the middle of the road near Seville, Spain read: THIS TREE HITS CARS ONLY IN SELF DEFENSE.

1060.   Sign stuck in the back window of a car with Georgia tags: AVOID HANGOVERS. STAY DRUNK.

1061. Sign at a restaurant: OUR STEAKS ARE SO TENDER WE WONDER HOW THE COW EVER WALKED.

1062. Sign in the parking lot of a South Dayton, Ohio Church: NO PARKING—VIOLATORS WILL BE BAPTIZED.

1063. Sign on a road in Biloxi, Mississippi: MAIN HIGHWAY OPEN FOR TRAFFIC WHILE DETOUR IS BEING RE-PAVED.

1064. Sign on a dryer at a North Dayton coin-operated laundry: WHEN YOU ARE FINISHED WASHING, PLEASE REMOVE ALL YOUR CLOTHES.

1065. Sign on the back of a car in Oklahoma City: PROMOTE BEEF. RUN OVER A CHICKEN.

1066. Sign in a supermarket: THIS PLACE IS GUARDED BY A SHOTGUN THREE NIGHTS A WEEK. YOU GUESS WHICH NIGHTS.

1067. Sign in a Lewisburg, Tennessee garage: OLD MUFFLERS NEVER DIE. THEY JUST GET EXHAUSTED.

1068. Neat sign outside a house: NOTICE: THIS LAWN DOES NOT FLUSH. DRAIN YOUR PET ELSEWHERE.

1069. Sign on a plumbing truck: TAKE US TO YOUR LEAKER.

1070. Sign in house window: PIANO FOR SALE.
Sign in window next door: HURRAH!

1071. Sign in a garage: DON'T SMOKE IN HERE. IF YOUR LIFE ISN'T WORTH ANYTHING, GASOLINE IS!

1072. Sign in a church: NO SMOKING! THOU SHALT NOT FLICK THY BIC.

1073. Sign in florist shop: SEND SOME FLOWERS TO YOUR HONEY. (AND DON'T FORGET YOUR WIFE.)

368, 412, 461, 501, 520, 1031

RX for That Ailing Speech

RX #69.   Occasionally a speaker will run into a situation that every platform personality dreads. A heckler in the audience. In the case of the nightclub comedian, a heckler can be handled by a number of "put downs" which have been prepared especially for such an occasion by the experienced professional who is not rattled by confrontation with an obnoxious character. This method of attack is not recommended for the average platform speaker. In the first place, he is generally not equipped with the ammunition to shoot down this verbal sniper. In the second place, it is not a high class way to handle a potentially embarrassing situation.

So what do you do? My advice is simple—ignore him or her. It is especially important not to even look at them if this is at all possible. Look over them, around them, in the opposite direction. This lets your audience know right away that you are still in command of the situation and you choose not to lower yourself to these kinds of tactics. The audience will be sympathetic with you and generally will take care of the heckler themselves. If you are confident, know your material extremely well, and appear to be non-plused, the audience will appreciate your efforts even more for showing courage in the face of adversity.

It is also important to keep thinking happy thoughts, keep smiling, keep talking. The heckler comes in many forms, not just a person who is trying to steal the spotlight. The heckler can be a person who is emotionally upset at the moment, a smart aleck, a radical, and perhaps the most common form of heckler—the drunk. All of them should be handled in a similar manner in my opinion—ignore them.

SINGERS

1074.   The woman showed up at church in a mini-mini skirt and sat in the front row. In a short while, the choir director leaned over to a member and asked, "Isn't that Fanny Green?" "Oh, no," the choir member replied, "it's the reflection of the light from the stained-glass window."

1075. "Now that you have heard my voice, what would you suggest to accompany me?" the singer asked. The impresario replied, "A bodyguard."

1076. ALAN KING complimented Lena Horne by saying, "When you sing, it sounds as if your larynx is wearing hot pants!"

1077. Enrico Caruso was appearing in an opera with a soprano who kept trying to upstage him. To the tenor who delighted in horseplay on the stage, this was a challenge to be cheerfully accepted. He waited for an opportunity to retaliate. It came late in the opera, when the soprano sang an aria in which she had to reach the real high notes. It was her habit, when singing this aria, to hold her hands in front of her, palms up and fingers intertwined. Then, as she strained for the top note, she would clasp her hands together until the knuckles were white. Caruso, standing at her side, watched as she approached the uppermost limits of her range. Then, just before they snapped shut, he dropped an egg into her hands.

SMALL TOWNS

1078. The city council in a small town moved to get tough on burglars. Anyone who had to be shot or shot at would be charged for the ammunition. A deputy shot a thief three times, apprehended him, charged him with burglary plus 75¢ for the three bullets ... He didn't have change for a dollar so the deputy shot him one more time.

1079.   My hometown is so small they use the Avon lady for the church bell.

1080.   If nobody knows the troubles you've seen, you don't live in a small town.

1081.   Our town is so small that it is the kind of place where the marshal has a five-cell flashlight and a one-cell jail.

1082.   The town is really small. A tourist bought a map of the place—and it doesn't even fold.

1083.   His hometown is so small that the only way they can get a Greyhound to stop there is to throw it a bone.

1084.   A small town is where anybody who has a better reputation than he deserves is probably a lot smarter than he is given credit for.

1085.   Excerpt from a wedding story that appeared in a small town newspaper: "This is the third marriage for the groom. He has also been through World War II."

1086.   Hear about the smallest town and the worst energy crisis? The lights dim when you use your electric typewriter.

1087.   An elderly cop in a small town spotted an old-timer in a Model T. Pulled him over to the side. When the old-timer started making excuses the cop said, "Relax friend, I just wanted to see what it felt like to put my foot on a running board again."

107, 433, 672, 979

RX for That Ailing Speech

RX #70.   The great performer, Carol Burnett, makes her art look effortless. She has the uncanny ability to make the audience feel that she is unconcerned with the events that unfold in her form of comedy. However, do not be deceived. Everyone who works with any form of humor must have a goal for themselves. It is obvious from the length of her stardom that her goals have served her well. I recall reading or hearing somewhere that Carol Burnett received her inspiration from some of her readings in Yoga. The goal is one which she doubted that she would ever reach—to become "untroubled by failure and untouched by triumph." Note that a goal does not have to be reached in order to remain a goal. It is unfortunate that we have to look to outside opinions for approval for our own happiness.

Life is full of peaks and valleys, but we must remember that it is up to us to be the masters of our fate, the captains of our destiny. If you feel destined to shed a ray of sunshine through joy and laughter in an otherwise troubled world, you can chart your own course and determine for yourself whether or not you have arrived safely in port. There will be times when your material will "bomb," there will also be times when you will be heralded as a genius in your performance. The point I'm making here is quite simple. Don't be discouraged by your failures; don't believe it when on some occasion you are lifted up as the best in the business. In many ways, failure is more important to you than success. Failure is a learning experience. Triumph is short-lived in the speaking business and must be repeated again and again if you are to develop as a humorous speaker. Accept your failures as an opportunity to become better, rejoice in your victories but try to remain humble by laughing it off. It's good advice.

SONS

1088. The father was lecturing his son on economy. "You know, son, when I was a boy there was a depression and my father didn't make much money. I didn't have half the things you do." "Well," replied the boy, "can I help it if my father is smarter than your father?"

1089.   After graduation from college, a young man was told by his father to clean out the silo. He balked. "Dad, I'm a college grad." "Oh, that's right, I forgot. Well, I'll come out and show you how."

1090.   There is a modern story to the effect that when Adam and his son Seth were taking a hike together, Seth noticed the beautiful Garden of Eden. "Father," Seth began, "that is a beautiful place so why don't we live there?" "My son," Adam replied, "we used to live there until your mother ate us out of house and home!"

1091.   "What is the difference between capital and labor?" Sam asked his father. "Well, son," the elder said, "the money you lend represents capital—and getting it back represents labor."

1092.   The wisened father down the street says he instructed his teenage son to cut the grass and the kid replied that grass cutting wasn't relevant. The boy asked, "What does mowing the lawn relate to in the overall scheme of things?" His dad gave this some thought and then replied, "It relates to whether or not you get any allowance this week."

1093.   A conscientious mother, keenly alert to current drug problems among our youth, was horrified by a note she found in her son's pocket. "Can you explain this?" she confronted him. "Puff, puff, drag, puff, puff, puff?" "Sure," the boy airily replied, "I'm learning *The Star Spangled Banner* on my harmonica."

1094.   My son let his hair down—and smothered.

1095.   My son took a girl home from a party the other night and it was real romantic. Her head was on his shoulder—and someone else was carrying her feet.

1096.   This dumb "right turn on red" thing! My son thinks it's so great, I swear he goes places he doesn't have to go just to take advantage of it.

1097. Anybody who thinks practice makes perfect doesn't have a son taking piano lessons.

1098. Dad: When I was a boy, I never told lies.
Son: When did you start?

1099. Fellow says insanity must run in the family. His son keeps writing home for money ... and he keeps sending it.

1100. Normal sons have an eight-track stereo and a one-track mind.

1101. I wouldn't call my son a liar. Let's just say he lives on the wrong side of the facts.

1102. "How come," asked my son, "it is insulting to tell someone he has a hole in his head, but complimentary to say he has an open mind?"

159, 197, 200, 201, 207, 217, 220, 222, 224, 225, 232, 233, 295, 301, 400, 536, 562, 662, 681, 774, 958, 972, 1004

RX for That Ailing Speech

RX #71. Some speakers feel they are not suited from a personality standpoint to use humor. Believe me, everyone has the capability to utilize comic relief in their presentation. In fact, humor has such therapeutic usefulness that it has been said that a person who cannot find any humor in most situations is either going to end up on a soapbox or at the psychiatrist's office. While this may be overstating the power of humor, it does lend credence to the thought that laughter, smiles, grins, chuckles or some variation thereof can be the balancing point for the well-adjusted speaker. Since we like to think that the average listener is also fairly well-adjusted, it just makes good sense to temper your serious thoughts with some light-hearted moments. If you will develop your presentation along the serious lines of thought that you wish to convey, then use this handbook to pump in some humor, you will discover one of the most useful techniques in communications.

SPEAKERS

1103. A public speaker once began by saying, "Ladies and Gentlemen! I trust I haven't omitted anyone."

1104. Most candidates aren't very exciting speakers. Their delivery is about as effective as the post office.

1105. Some speakers talk so fast they can be compared to a man reading Playboy with his wife turning the pages.

1106. Instruments are currently used that will throw a speaker's voice more than a mile. Now we need an instrument that will throw the speaker an equal distance.

1107. "You were much better than our last speaker. He talked for an hour and never said anything. You took only 15 minutes."

1108. The hardest thing for a speaker to remember during an introduction is not to nod his head in agreement when the toastmaster praises him.

1109. Veteran GEORGE BURNS insists his work is difficult: "People think it's easy to stand up here and tell jokes. Well, it's not. Every year it becomes more of an effort to stand up."

1110. BOB HOPE: "I was here last year and came back to hatch the egg I laid."

548, 925, 964, 976, 1005, 1242

SPORTS

1111. A basketball official was jeered by a man in the crowd. He stopped the game, sat next to the man, blew his whistle and yelled, "Play ball ... if you can call 'em from up here, so can I."

1112. I played golf next to Jack Nicklaus. At least I think it was him. After I hit the ball, he said, "Boy, if you're a golfer, I'm Jack Nicklaus!"

1113. Known far and wide for his optimism, a small-time little league coach entered the locker room and gave the players a pre-game pep talk. "All right, boys," he explained cheerily, "here we are, unbeaten, untied, and unscored upon and ready for the first game of the season."

1114. Do you know what women playing tennis reminds me of? Take away the rackets and the balls, and they look like mothers trying to keep the kids in the yard.

1115. Our baseball fans are so tough that if a game is rained out, they go to the airport and boo bad landings.

1116. A constant watcher of football games on TV went to have his eyes examined. As the doctor put the light on his eyeballs, the patient asked him if he saw any cataracts. "No," the doctor replied, "just yard markers."

1117. Last year 15,000 accidents occurred on the nation's golf courses. And that doesn't include holes-in-one.

RX for That Ailing Speech

RX #72. It is a common misconception throughout the world that all speakers are expected to be dull. Whenever you enliven a meeting with your humorous remarks and insights, you can expect the crowd to react favorably. Many speakers are able to do this in their platform presentation, but then they fall short in what is commonly known as a question/answer session. You can maintain the levity of your remarks by the simple process of anticipating the types of questions that may be asked and having more humorous remarks to follow up your original presentation. This will make you appear to be a genuinely humorous person when you have merely capitalized on human nature and the natural thought process.

Any thinking person can generally anticipate 50 percent or more of the questions that will be asked on the subject that he or she covers. If, for instance, you are asked the question, "How does your company's product rank with its competition?" You might be prepared to answer, "Just a little below General Motors but somewhat higher than Tinker Toys." Learn to anticipate questions and be ready with some witty responses before launching into a hard sales pitch for your product or idea and you will find the audience much more receptive to you and your product.

In many instances, especially in the case of free speakers, the club or association customarily awards a certificate or plaque to the individual for having spoken. If you anticipate this happening you can really put the final touches on a good presentation by humbly accepting this honor by putting yourself down as well as building up the award at the same time. Try something like, "This is the nicest award I have ever received. I have only been honored once before and that was by a Ghetto Association in downtown Chicago. They voted me man-of-the-year but instead of receiving a plaque, an artist spray-painted my name on the wall of a subway." Learn to anticipate events for an extension of the good-natured humor that you will be able to employ.

* * * * * *

1118.   A coach, explaining why the team will not pray

before games this year: "We've got so many things to pray for, we'd be penalized for delay of game."

1119.   A local coach has a novel way of picking his backs and linemen.

> "I just take them into the woods and turn them loose," he says.
> "The ones who run around the trees become backs and the ones who run over the trees become linemen."

1120.   There's a form of Russian Roulette where you put six cobras in a room and play the flute. One of the cobras is deaf.

152, 695

STUDENTS

1121.   Some students drink at the fountain of knowledge, others just gargle.

1122.   I guess you heard about the computer report on the student body of a certain college: "48 percent of the students are male, 47 percent female, and 5 percent undecided."

1123.   New law students stood before their law professor for the first day's classes. "You are about to embark on a course of study that will try your very souls. Some of you will make it and some of you will crack. A few of you will go on to bigger and better things. Those who crack will be lawyers."

1124.   *Student's Motto:*
> Now I lay me down to rest.
> I pray to pass tomorrow's test.
> If I should die before I wake,
> That's one less test
> I'll have to take.

1125.   Coed: "With this hectic college life, don't you wish you were a barefoot boy again?"

Student: "Not me, I was raised on a chicken farm."

16, 951, 1142

SUCCESS

1126.   REDD FOXX: "Success hasn't changed me. I'm still eating soul food—only now I don't owe for it."

1127.   A successful man is one who can make more money than his wife can spend. A successful woman is one who can find such a man.

1128.   A man became a success because of his ugly wife. He kept a picture of her on his desk and it made him stay and work overtime.

1129.   Behind every successful man stands another guy trying to take his place!

1130.   A successful man is a fellow just like you who worked harder.

1131.   He had an ancestor who came to this country and made a success even though he knew only three words of English: "Stick 'em up!"

1132.   You're not really successful until someone claims they sat beside you in grade school.

799

RX for That Ailing Speech

RX #73.   Take a tip from some of the masters of comedy writing. A rule of thumb among the writers for *The Tonight Show* is to feel they have had a very productive day if four out of each one hundred jokes they write are selected for use by the host of the show. This means that even among professionals, only four percent of their material at first glance is considered good enough to get a response from the average audience. Even then, they realize that the audience will be the final judge, and that four percent may drop even more once an audience reacts.

Among these top professionals, even failure of their accepted material is taken with a grin. The writers, it is rumored, have a saying when something is not received in a favorable light by an audience. The saying is, "It was funny when it left here." The moral is to keep plugging away until your material has had a chance to be tested again and again. Of course, the final judge is the listener but you should always start out with material that to you is "funny when it left here."

TAXES

1133. A taxpayer recently moaned: "I owe the government so much money, they don't know whether to throw me in jail or recognize me as a foreign power.

1134. Luxury is any bare necessity, plus tax.

1135. They've changed the IRS to Eternal Revenue Service. The tax boys follow into the next world.

1136. Ask not what your country can do for you; if you do, you are sure to be taxed for it.

1137. Patrick Henry ought to come back and see what taxation WITH representation is like.

1138. Two sneakiest words in the English language: PLUS TAX.

1139. There are two kinds of tax collectors: Those who think they are God and those who are sure of it.

1140. Internal Revenue man eyeing taxpayer's expense claims: "Shall we go over it item by item, or would you prefer to chicken out right now?"

538, 971, 1183

TEACHERS

1141. A teacher was telling her husband about the excitement when classes dismissed for the summer vacation. She said, "There was foot-stomping, table-banging and all-around rejoicing." "Real wild, huh," commented the husband who had lived with nine months of nightly reports on conduct in the classroom. "It sure was wild!" his teacher-wife agreed, adding, "and that was just in the teachers' lounge."

1142. During a lecture on science, the teacher asked one student, "This gas contains poison. What steps would you take if it should by chance escape?" "Long ones," came the reply.

1143. A realistic, concerned teacher shook up her third-graders the other day: "If you don't learn to write your name, when you grow up you'll have to pay cash for everything."

1144. A note from teacher: "Dear Parents, if you promise not to believe all your child says happens at school, I'll promise not to believe all he says happens at home."

1145. Recalling MARK TWAIN: "To be good is noble. But to teach others how to be good is nobler—and less trouble."

1146. It's hard to be a schoolteacher. Decisions, decisions—like whether the kid who can't see the blackboard needs glasses or a haircut.

1147. The Sunday school teacher instructed her pupils: "Study this picture of Lot and his family. He is being told to take his wife and daughter and flee from Sodom. Now, children, can you see anything else?" One spoke up immediately, "I can see everything except the flea."

> **16, 206, 214, 223, 411, 539, 550, 554, 560, 1007**

RX for That Ailing Speech

RX #74. The art of adding mythical humor to an otherwise perfectly legitimate story is truly an art. However, it is an art that can be learned. Simply jot down the ideas you intend to convey but leave enough space, on paper, between the ideas so that some humorous lines can also be noted to weave into the fabric of the remarks of a humorous interpretation to hold the attention of your audience.

As an example, an economist might outline the economic cycles of the past in order to compare them to current economic events. In outlining the events of the Great Depression, an economist might add, "While my father was not an economist, he was a very astute businessman. He had the foresight to beat the depression of 1929. He went broke in 1928. While some criticized his inability to even balance his checkbook, he was one of the few men to have the foresight to be overdrawn when Roosevelt closed the banks." Weaving humor into the fabric of a speech is no more difficult than weaving a piece of cloth. It just takes a little understanding, a little organization and a little planning. Your effort may just be a finished product that people will look at and say, "Gee, that's a nice fit."

TELEPHONES

1148. Alexander Graham Bell gave us the telephone. Teenagers gave us the busy signal.

1149. Alexander Graham Bell would never have invented the telephone had he had a teenage daughter.

1150. My wife talks so much, I have to have the telephone refinished every two months.

1151. The old-fashioned wall telephone had its advantages. For instance, a woman quit talking when her feet got tired.

1152. His telephone bill is terrific. Last month he had calls to Phoenix, Chicago and New York. Don't you have any friends in the state?

1153. Our family doctor is convinced there isn't any life in outer space— "It isn't listed on my daughter's telephone bill."

1154. When thou art in the bathtub, ask not for whom the phone ringest, for thou knowest that it ringest for thee.

1155. He's so honest you could shoot dice with him over the telephone.

1156. The man walked into a public place with both ears bandaged. Someone had to ask why. He explained, "I am watching the basketball game on TV and my wife is ironing nearby. She leaves for a moment, placing the iron on the board, and the phone rings. I grab the hot iron and put it to my ear, thinking it is the telephone." "But what happened to the other ear?" "I hadn't any more than hung up when the man calls back."

1157. The father of five teenagers alleges that it's been six years since he picked up a telephone in his house that wasn't warm.

1158. A Chinese telephone company was preparing to publish a directory. They finally abandoned the project when it was discovered there were thousands of Wings and Wongs, and this would result in too much winging the wong number.

1159.   The father of the household called the telephone company and ordered a 50-foot extension cord put on the phone. He explained, "I want my daughter to stay outside more now that the weather is nice."

1160.   Trying to locate her boyfriend in a distant army camp, a girl called on the long distance operator for help. "What outfit is he in?" asked the operator. "In his fatigues I think," was the answer. "He's on KP."

1161.   RODNEY DANGERFIELD: "I met one girl at a dance. I figured I'd get her phone number. The most she would give me was her area code."

1162.   The bathtub was invented in 1850 and the telephone in 1875. If you had been living in 1850, you could have sat in the tub for 25 years without the phone ringing.

191, 246, 405, 423, 588, 727, 992

RX for That Ailing Speech

RX #75.   One technique a good humorist uses is to personalize his remarks so that they appear to have been tailor-made for the group he is addressing. Bob Hope is a master of this technique. It appears that every remark he makes has been specially prepared for the group he is addressing. In reality, he and his writers have merely made jokes that conform to the situation. For example, you might want to relate to your audience the great discovery of a mythical archaeologist who recently confided in you that he had discovered a matriarchal society where women rule and men are nothing. When you asked him to identify the place, he replied, "In Cincinnati." This line could be used again and again, successfully, by merely changing the name of the town to conform to the place, or a nearby place, where you are speaking.

TELEVISION

1163. I don't allow my wife to stay up and watch the late show. It makes her sleepy on her paper route.

1164. The husband was curious. "Why do you sniff and weep at a movie over the imaginary woes of people you never met?" The wife replied, "For the same reason you scream and yell when a man you don't know slides into second base."

1165. First television gives you a headache, then sells you something to relieve it.

1166. FRED ALLEN once gave his explanation of why people preferred TV to radio: "They'd rather look at something bad than hear something good."

1167. Nothing makes a mother's day longer than waiting for the TV repairman.

1168. We can expect it any day: A television set with a double screen. This will enable the studio to broadcast both a program and a commercial continuously.

1169. The boss ate so many TV dinners he broke out in a test pattern.

1170. We bought two portable television sets with rabbit ears. Now they have multiplied to 36 sets.

1171. Which is more important—television or newspaper? The newspaper, of course. You can't put a TV camera in the bottom of a birdcage when you're through with it.

1172. Actor Burt Reynolds made a somewhat inauspicious return to his south Georgia hometown when a tire on the beatup film car he was driving went flat. Reynolds engineered the auto to a local garage. "You sure look familiar," the mechanic told him, "Haven't I seen you before?" "Maybe at your local theater," Reynolds suggested. "Maybe," said the mechanic, "where do you usually sit?"

1173.   My kid is so hooked on TV violence, he eats popcorn out of a shoulder holster.

1174.   Early to bed and early to rise—and you'll certainly miss a lot of rotten TV shows.

1175.   Someday they will invent a TV set that interferes with your neighbor's power tools.

1176.   If the Lord had expected us to watch so much TV, he'd have given us square eyeballs.

1177.   Sooner or later there will be a TV sportscaster's head on Mount Rushmore even if they have to enlarge the mountain or shrink the head.

205, 215, 295, 447, 667, 784

RX for That Ailing Speech

RX #76.   Realism and a sincere expression are essential to good humor. It is a technique to grab the audiences' imagination and make them ponder "Well now, could this be true?" A good example that could be used in historical circles, perhaps in the study of some legendary character who helped to develop your part of the country through his initiative, might be expressed in a few lines that are a mixture of truth and humor.

For instance, "As you know, the man for whom this town was named got his start in a questionable manner. One of the first settlers in this county was a businessman with high initiative. It is well-known that he started out with only two cows and a bull. From this meager beginning he developed an empire. My great, great uncle started out the same way but his career was cut short by his inability to keep his business principle a secret from the competition. Uncle Fred also started out with a couple of cows and a bull. Each cow had ten or twelve calves a year. His competition didn't complain very much until the bull started having calves too. Then the vigilantes made it so disagreeable that Uncle Fred finally had to quit the business to go into road construction. Even there he used such primitive tools that he couldn't get ahead. His sledge hammer kept getting tangled up in red tape and leg. irons. However, Uncle Fred was a pioneer of sorts. He helped to establish a dress code that lasted for many, many years. Long before it became popular, he wore his hair very short and dressed in very loud clothing." The crowd is able to honor one man for his pioneering spirit and laugh at another for going to jail for cattle rustling.

TIME

1178. Time hangs heaviest for these: A boy waiting to catch his first fish, a wife waiting for her husband to come home, a husband waiting for his wife on a windy street corner and many a candidate on election night.

1179. Any time you're trying to finish something, why is it there are so many last minute details and so few last minutes?

1180. A woman reports that she wants to read a new book, *How To Get Control of Your Time and Life,* just as soon as she finds the time.

1181. The local pharmacist is just recuperating from having to set all the tiny time pills in cold capsules ahead an hour.

1182. Hear about the Egyptian mummy ... that was pressed for time?

1183. There is a time and place for everything? Not so. There is no time when it's convenient to pay taxes and no place where you can enjoy the company of a skunk.

1184.   Second thoughts are always best—the problem is to get them to arrive on time.

319, 716

VOTING

1185.   A frightening thought is that if the majority is nuts, it is the sane who are committed to the hospital.

1186.   It's hard to say which is worse—the pre-election oratory or the post-election analysis.

1187.   A key slogan in a recent election— "What You Vote for Today, You Live with Tomorrow"—produced 35,197 write-in votes for Raquel Welch.

1188.   "What did you think of the two candidates?"
"I'm glad only one was elected!"

1189.   Fifty percent of all accidents happen around the home—the other half in voting booths.

WAITERS

1190.   Patron: "Waiter, what's this fly doing in my soup?"
Waiter: "Offhand I'd say the backstroke, sir."

1191.   "Waiter, this steak is so tough I can't eat it!"
"Then get out! This is no place for weaklings!"

1192.   Man, dining out, told his waiter, "Put the rest of my steak in a bag for my dog, will you? ... and put in a few slices of bread in case he wants to make a sandwich."

1193.   A man, leaving a cafe said, "Waiter, I find that I have just enough money to pay for the dinner, but I have nothing in the way of a tip for you." "Let me add up that bill again, sir," replied the waiter.

1194.   At a restaurant two little old ladies asked the waiter to explain what a martini was. He replied, "It's gin and vermouth, served with an olive or twist." The ladies conferred, then one said, "We don't want the gin and vermouth, but bring us two Oliver Twists."

297, 1038

RX for That Ailing Speech

RX #77.   It should be kept in mind that the most effective use of humor is not simply to make an audience laugh or to entertain them but to make them see the significance of a certain point. Of course, there are times when you will simply want to entertain an audience with escapism. This is generally the role of the comic, but the humorist prefers to use wit to emphasize reality. A well-placed, properly timed gag can do more to grab the attention of your audience than all the eloquence that the average speaker can muster.

For example, "Several years ago Congress passed what is known as the Fair Credit Reporting Act. The act specifically states that a credit reporting agency, in connection with an application for credit or employment, may not contain reference to convictions for certain offenses after a period of seven years. A convicted robber, for instance, who has maintained a clean record for a period of seven years after release from prison is entitled to have a credit report that makes no mention of his previous trial or convictions. While I realize that no law is completely free of loopholes, there is at least one injustice in this law. After seven years, a murderer, robber or burglar can have his record cleared. But you can attend the State University for just one semester and it stays on your record forever."

This is a great way to "grab" an audience with humor. As soon as everybody starts laughing, the ones who may not have been paying attention will start asking themselves, "What did I miss?" Then their subconscious mind will quickly review what has just been said and the use of the parable has enhanced retention of the moral. It becomes a sort of instant replay to the mind.

WAITRESSES

1195. HENNY YOUNGMAN: "A guy goes into a French restaurant, orders dinner, waitress disappears for an hour. Guy screams GENDARME! Waitress comes and says, 'Gendarme means Policeman.' Guy says, 'Yeah, I know. There's a hold-up in the kitchen. Go get my food.'"

1196. The waitress at the local cafe isn't too sharp. A customer asked for coffee without cream and she told him: "We don't have a drop of cream in the house—how about having it without milk?"

1197. Said the cute little waitress, slipping up beside the customer: "I've got deviled kidneys, calves' brains, pigs' feet, chicken livers, and..." "Forget it, sister," replied the customer, "I've got a headache, eczema, fallen arches, corns, a bunion, three warts, and an empty stomach. Tell your troubles to someone else, and bring me some ham and eggs."

1198. Restaurant patron: "Two eggs, please. Don't fry them a second after the white is cooked. Don't turn them over. Not too much grease. Just a pinch of salt. No pepper. Well, waitress, what are you waiting for?" Waitress: "The hen's name is Eleanor—is that all right?"

1027, 1039, 1043

WEATHER

1199. A visitor back from Ireland recalled an old

description of the weather there: "If you can see the top of the mountain, it's going to rain. And if you can't see the top, it *is* raining."

1200. "How did you find the weather while you were away?"

"Oh, I just went outside and there it was!"

1201. It only rained twice last week. Once for three days and once for four days.

1202. Local weather forecasters hesitate to call it rain. They prefer to call it dew. A friend stepped off his front porch this morning and they're dragging the dew for his body.

1203. Weatherman to radio announcer: "Better break it to 'em gently. Just say, 'Partly cloudy with scattered showers followed by a hurricane.'"

WEIGHT WATCHERS

1204. Bum: "Can you spare 50 cents? I haven't eaten in four days."

Weight watcher: "Gosh, I wish I had your willpower."

1205. Uncle Fred has finally been stimulated to go on a diet. He was out at the auction barn the other day and a fellow gave him a duck. Uncle Fred, who weighs over 300 pounds, had this duck under his arm. Another farmer yelled out, "Hey, where did you get that pig?" Uncle Fred said, "This ain't no pig, this is a duck." The guy said, "I wasn't talking to you. I was talking to that duck."

1206. Somebody ought to write a new book on the jogging craze and call it *Physical Fitness in a Sagging Society.*

1207. A friends' wife went on a diet. He says she just

throws everything in a blender and drinks it. He has been on the same diet without knowing exactly what he was consuming. He quit inquiring after he asked the first time and found that for lunch that day he drank a chicken.

1208.   Forty years of neglect can't be cured by an 18-hour girdle.

1209.   Here's the latest in diet drinks: You mix two jiggers of Scotch to one jigger of Metrecal. So far I've lost five pounds and my driver's license.

RX for That Ailing Speech

RX #78.   Nick Arnold has been a top comedy writer ten years for such well-known programs as *The Tonight Show* and others. As a victim of cerebral palsy, Nick has an obvious disadvantage in speaking to an audience, and yet he is a popular speaker. During an interview on Tom Snyder's television show, he was asked the question, "Do people ever laugh *at* you?" His answer was a marvelous study in the way a well-balanced individual reacts to adversity. "No, I let them know in the first few minutes that I know that they know and it's all right to laugh. I've never had a bad experience." He went on to relate one of the stories he uses to illustrate the fact. "I tell people that I was called by the U.S. Army for a physical. After they finished with me, I was given the classification of 5-E. That means 'Don't come unless we're invaded.'"

One lady who caught his act, thought it was just that—an act. She followed him outside the nightclub where he performed. Nick continued to act in a way that is characteristic of cerebral palsy victims, that is he could not completely control all of his muscles in the way that has come to represent normal function. He continued to convulse the lady with his incoordinated gestures and humorous barbs, which led her to remark in parting, "It's amazing how you stay in character."

This should be a lesson to all of us that no matter what difficulty we face in our personal lives, a sense of humor can be utilized to provide a more pleasant environment for all. Now aren't you ashamed of your little hangups because you are afraid that everything won't turn out just perfect? So what if you are bald, ugly, short, fat? Blame it on your wife, unless you're a woman. Then you had better really have a sense of humor.

* * * * * *

1210.   My wife disguises the taste of her reducing pills. She crushes them and sprinkles them on a hot fudge sundae!

1211.   I am on a severe diet. I only eat on the days the mayor is in town.

1212.   Millie was standing on the bathroom scale when she muttered, "How can I lose all this weight?" Fred told her to stand there for three days.

1213.   A man and his wife went shopping for a man's suit and as the salesman measured the husband's waist, she remarked, "It's amazing when you realize a coconut palm that wide at the bottom would be at least 90 feet tall."

1214.   Description of a fat friend: "He has more chins than a Chinese phone book."

1215.   A fat man who likes himself just the way he is says, "If the Lord meant us to be on our toes all the time, he wouldn't have given us so much to sit down with."

1216.   A fat kid had to quit exercising on a pogo stick. It measured six on the Richter scale.

1217.   Some people grow up and spread cheer. Others just grow up and spread.

1218.   Overheard: "My wife is wide awake. But without her girdle she's even wider asleep."

1219.   Some stretch pants have no other choice.

1220.   Hear about the fellow suffering from Dunlap Disease? His belly done lapped over his belt.

1221.   A sure-fire way for all you chubbies to reduce is the Good News Diet. You only eat when the news is good.

WIVES

1222.   Do you realize you get more protection when you acquire a car than when you acquire a wife? Think about it. When have you ever heard of a wife being recalled for defective parts?

1223.   Her husband says he still remembers the first time he met her: "Bells rang, lights flashed—she was playing the slot machine."

1224.   A mute couple could communicate with one another only through sign language. One night he stayed out until the wee hours, and she, waiting for him, grew angrier by the minute. When he finally staggered in, she let him know how she felt, her fingers flying a mile a minute. Then, just as he began to reply, she turned off the lights.

RX for That Ailing Speech

RX #79.   In our search for humor, we often overlook one of the best sources of mirth. That is, everyday conversations. A case in point is a joke that I am told started out originally as a witty remark by someone in the audience. The story is told about a county-wide play that depicted the life of Christ. Competition was fierce throughout the county for the various parts that were available, of which there were many. One little town only had one participant to make the grade and he was chosen to play the part of Judas. The town was extremely proud of their contribution, but when the reviews on the play were released through the newspapers, rave reports were given to many, many actors but not one single mention of the character who played Judas. At a local service club, a speaker was lamenting the fact that this deserving individual was completely overlooked and he thought it was an over-sight of the greatest magnitude. Some wise cracker in the audience made a suggestion to a nearby table that the error could be corrected by simply having the local newspaper editor, who was a member of the club, to print a headline in the next edition, LOCAL BOY BETRAYS CHRIST. Keep your ears open for these kinds of remarks and you will continue to add to your repertory of effective humor.

* * * * * *

1225.   Joe's wife used to be a cover girl in Dallas—she put the lids on the sewer.

1226.   A rather cynical fellow was told by his wife that she would dance on his grave...at which time he arranged for a burial at sea.

1227.   My wife is so dumb. She thought Cheerios were doughnut seeds.

1228.   My barber says his wife has a compartment in her purse which she calls the "Bermuda Triangle" because things drop into it and are never seen again.

1229.   My wife got a two-day mud pack beauty treatment. She was absolutely beautiful for two days...then the mud fell off.

1230.   If you have a waterbed, the first thing to look for in a wife is short toenails.

1231.   "My wife's cooking melts in your mouth," the young husband said. "She never thaws it long enough."

1232.   My wife's such a bad cook that she prepares a nice dinner by putting a large roast beef and a small roast beef in the oven at the same time. When the small one is burnt to a crisp, she knows the large one is just right.

1233. RODNEY DANGERFIELD: "I didn't get no respect even on my wedding night. My wife told me we were seeing too much of each other."

1234. "Your wife can fix meal in a jiffy?"
"Yeah, McDonalds and Dairy Queen are across the street."

1235. The reason Solomon had so many wives was because he wanted at least one to be in good humor when he came home.

> **17, 31, 97, 164, 166, 174, 177, 248, 280, 305, 307, 310, 355, 377, 385, 515, 616, 625, 635, 638, 641, 645, 653, 710, 739, 752, 791, 795, 1008, 1024, 1073, 1105, 1128, 1150, 1163, 1210, 1218**

WOMEN

1236. ERMA BOMBECK: "What is faster than a speeding bullet? More powerful than a locomotive? Able to leap tall buildings in a single jump? Women at garage sales, that's who."

1237. The woman motorist, on her trip through Europe, posed for a souvenir snapshot next to an historic ruin in Greece. "Don't get the car in the picture," she cautioned. "My husband will be certain I ran into the place."

1238. A man lay in the middle of the street, flat on his stomach, wriggling convulsively. A number of people stood by helplessly until a flustered woman pushed her way through the crowd. "Why isn't someone helping this poor man?" she exclaimed. "Can't you see he's suffering?" When she got no answer from the spectators, she grabbed the man, turned him over on his back, and began to administer mouth-to-mouth resuscitation. He began to squirm and when he finally got his mouth free, he said, "Lady, I don't know what you think you're doing...but I'm trying to fish my hat out of that manhole."

1239. A woman always had something good to say about everyone, no matter who it might be. "I do believe you'd say something good about the devil," a friend told her. "Well, he is persistent," she said.

RX for That Ailing Speech

RX #80. One subject that I have scarcely touched during the discourse in this handbook is the art of storytelling. This has been a purposeful omission so that you might have the maximum amount of humorous material with the minimum of direction. This lack of direction has also been on purpose in order to encourage you to add your own details. A developing storyteller will find ways to express himself and thereby utilize the ideas found in the handbook to make a unique presentation of his own design.

However, if you are inclined to lean toward yarn-spinning, there are certain vital qualities of a storyteller that should be kept in mind. The storyteller is one who truly wants to share, to give something, to divide his mirth and enjoy it with other people. A story needs detail. It puts meat on the skeleton, blood in the meat and salt in the blood. Also keep in mind that the best stories always spring out of the occasion at hand.

For instance, I once heard a speaker describe in vivid detail the plight of the poor and uneducated poverty-stricken rural population of India. He explained the anguish of the over-crowded country, the lack of knowledge in the field of birth control and the strong religious convictions of the Indian people for the production of human life. Children were encouraged to marry at an early age in order to produce more hands to work the fields to produce more food for an ever-increasing population. It became an endless cycle of supply and demand with the demand always outstripping the supply. "The anguish," he explained, "is accelerated by forced contact through an overpopulated concentration of people. While familiarity is not a bad thing on the surface, I might quote Mark Twain who said 'Familiarity breeds contempt—and children.'"

By adding his own details and building a vivid picture in the mind of his audience, this speaker was able to drive home a significant point through the use of a humorous, but often true, remark. Learn to add your own details to become a good storyteller. Then search this handbook for specific remarks that will add that special touch.

*   *   *   *   *   *

1240. Man to Southern Belle, "How did you get that gorgeous all-over tan?"
"Why, I just did everything under the sun."

1241. Two males were discussing moving some office furniture when a female co-worker interrupted. "If you wanted an expert on moving furniture why didn't you ask a woman?" she asked. "Because," one of the men said, "we only wanted to move it once."

1242. A speaker was lecturing on Persia before a group of women. He said men in Persia were inconsiderate and mistreated their wives, even making them work hard in the fields. "Why," he said, "you often see a woman and jackass hitched up together." From the audience a woman shouted, "That's not so unusual. You often see it over here."

1243. An Arab Sheik maintained his harem about five miles away from his house. Every night it was the custom of the Sheik to have his faithful servant dash over to the harem and bring back one of the lovelies. The Sheik lived to be 90 and the servant keeled over when he was 40. Moral: Women won't kill you; it's the running after them that does.

1244. This conversation was overheard in the ladies room of a plush country club. "Well, I wouldn't go so far as to say she's so wealthy she has servants, but her home is quite elegant and she's the only one I know of with a riding vacuum cleaner."

1245. A woman grew more and more frustrated as the line of cars behind her became longer after her auto had stalled and she could not restart the engine. At last she got out of the car, walked back to the first driver, and said: "I'm very sorry. I just can't seem to get my car started. If you'll go up there and give it a try, I'll stay here and blow your horn."

1246. A man spotted a young woman futilely edging in and out of a tiny parking space. Ten minutes later, thanks to his directions, the car was neatly parked in the space. "Thank you very much," the woman said, "but I was trying to get out."

1247. A woman declared she was going to fire her maid for taking off with two of her towels. "Which towels did she steal?" asked her husband. "The ones we got from that hotel in Las Vegas."

1248. A local Phyllis Diller-type got up late one morning. She had her hair in curlers, face in cold cream, body in a ragged house coat and feet in fuzzy, pink slippers. Her husband, in a rush too, had forgotten to take out a smelly bag of fish remains. Looking out the window, she spotted the city dump truck about to depart from the collection point. Just as the truck was lurching forward, she ran up behind it and yelled to a fellow in the back,

"Yohoo, am I too late for the garbage." He grinned and yelled back, "No, lady, hop right in."

1249. Women are like newspapers,
They have great forms, they
enjoy the last word, their
back numbers are not in demand, you
can't believe anything they say, and
every man should have his own and try
not to borrow his neighbor's.

1250. A police officer pulled a woman over to the curb and implied that her signals were confusing. "First you put your hand out as if you were going to turn left, then you waved your hand up and down, and then you turned right." The woman explained, "I decided not to turn left and when my hand was going up and down, I was erasing the left turn."

12, 22, 92, 303, 394, 397, 406, 456, 503, 631, 651, 1001, 1151

RX for That Ailing Speech

RX #81. Almost every speaker has had the experience of making a speech and immediately afterwards having someone take him off to one side to share a tale that one of your stories may have triggered in his mind. It is important to listen to these stories even if you may have heard them before. Not only is it a courtesy on your part to hear the person out who was kind enough to be stimulated to want to share something with you but you may also hear a different twist to a joke that you had never heard before. In addition, occasionally someone in the audience will actually come up with an original thought which occurred to him as you spoke.

For instance, I use a story that concerns an American Indian standing on one side of a babbling brook sending to his sweetheart on the other side the well-known love call of his tribe. Then I grab the microphone and breathe heavily into it. The crowd always laughs.

On one occasion after having told the story in this fashion, a sweet little old lady expressed something that seemed so out of character that it completely brought the house down for those who were gathered around close enough to hear. "I was thinking," she said, "when you told the story of the brave giving his love call, that you could have added another line. 'All his breath came in short pants.'" I added the line to my story, with her permission, and have continued to get an even bigger laugh than the one I had originally planned. The moral is that humor is kind of like sourdough, if you will continue to use it, it will continue to grow for you.

Index

NOTE: NUMBERS REFER TO JOKE
NUMBERS, NOT PAGE NUMBERS.

Pantyhose, 266, 472
Paper route, 1163
Parents, 218
Parking, 1246
Parking lot, 50
Parrot, 75
Partner, 159
Payments, 258
Pedestrians, 186
Pegasus, 71
Persistence, 1239
Pessimist, 418, 797, 798, 842
Pharmacist, 806, 1181
Philosopher, 668
Photos, 240
Piano, 1070, 1097
Piano tuner, 533
Pigeon, 122, 123
Pigs, 386
Plastic surgery, 256, 478
Plumber, 290
Poison ivy, 121
Pontiacs, 96
Porcupine, 109, 111
Postal rates, 609, 613
Potato, 119
Praise, 934
Prayer, 214, 216, 255
Pregnancy, 226, 303
Price tags, 936
Prosperity, 53, 874
Punishment, 219

Q

Quitter, 529

R

Rabbit, 64
Rain, 217, 1199, 1201, 1202
Recession, 344
Recipes, 242, 244, 248, 323
Reducing pills, 1210
Reunions, 15
Rolls Royce, 96
Romance, 413
Rooster, 110
"Roots," 427
Rubber tree, 115

S

Safe, 155
Safety belt, 176
Salad, 363
Salary, 666
Sales, 3, 7
Selling, 374
Sex education, 622
Sheep, 1050
Sheets, 93
Sheik, 92, 96, 97, 1243
Shower, 36
Shyness, 423
Skis, 7
Skunk, 114
Smog, 161
Smoking, 6, 288, 813, 814, 837, 1071, 1072
Social Security number, 24
Solar energy, 95, 921
Spelling, 157
Spinster, 5, 615
Sponge, 119
Stamps, 602, 603, 605
Statue, 122
Stealing, 1247
Stock market, 823, 922
Stupidity, 924
Subscriptions, 559
Surgery, 256, 308, 458, 478
Sweeteners, 1046, 1047
Swimming lessons, 817
Swordfish, 124

T

Tactless person, 802
Tan, 1240
Tardiness, 540
Tax refund, 334
Teenagers, 38, 173, 910, 1148, 1149, 1157
Temptation, 928
Testimony, 31
Thanksgiving, 84, 125
Toothpaste, 271
Toupee, 705
Tranquilizers, 629
Tree surgeon, 124